Riding the Elephant

blue
rider
press

CRAIG FERGUSON

Riding the Elephant

A MEMOIR OF
ALTERCATIONS,
HUMILIATIONS,
HALLUCINATIONS,
AND
OBSERVATIONS

Blue Rider Press
NEW YORK

blue
rider
press

An imprint of Penguin Random House LLC
penguinrandomhouse.com

Previously published as a Blue Rider Press hardcover: May 2019

The Library of Congress has cataloged the hardcover edition as follows:

Names: Ferguson, Craig, 1962– author.
Title: Riding the elephant : a memoir of altercations, humiliations,
hallucinations, and observations / Craig Ferguson.
Description: New York, New York : Blue Rider Press,
an imprint of Penguin Random House LLC, [2019]
Identifiers: LCCN 2018045212| ISBN 9780525533917 (hardcover) |
ISBN 9780525533931 (ebook)
Subjects: LCSH: Ferguson, Craig, 1962– | Television personalities—
United States—Biography. | Comedians—United States—Biography. |
Actors—United States—Biography.
Classification: LCC PN1992.4.F47 A3 2019 | DDC 791.4502/8092 [B]—dc23
LC record available at https://lccn.loc.gov/2018045212

Printed in the United States of America
1   3   5   7   9   10   8   6   4   2

Book design by Francesca Belanger

Blue Rider Press paperback ISBN: 9780525533924

CONTENTS

INTRODUCTION

*F*rom backstage I watched the tape run for the last show's introduction. I always assumed it was tape, even though it probably hadn't been for years. Tape is a thing of the past, a relic, redundant—exactly how I should have felt at that moment. My time was up. I had done ten years, it was someone else's problem now. I should have been sad, even just a little, a touch of bittersweet melancholy at least. I had certainly experienced those feelings on the run-up to the show's ending, but in that moment I wasn't sad, not even a little bit. It felt like the last day of my grim high school. I was elated. I felt the fog clearing. Finally I'd be able to see the horizon, get my bearings, and continue the journey.

The tape ended and both drummers thundered out the beat. I walked out, waved to the audience, and climbed on top of that fucking desk to sing the last song. I stomped in time, doing what I have always tried to do: attempting to follow the beat while trashing the varnish.

I have never thought of myself as a late-night talk show host. I've said that often to anyone who would listen, but I suppose it was a bit confusing, since all they knew about me was that I hosted a late-night talk show. The press was convinced that I was crushed not to be taking over for David Letterman when I left *The Late Late Show* in 2014, despite my public insistence since 2005, when I started in late night—often quoted in their very publications—that I didn't want the job. I didn't and I don't. You can check this online if you want, although I can't think why you'd bother at this point. Certainly nobody seemed to find it necessary at the time.

It seems to me people make up stories to fit their perception about you. They don't just do it about me, of course. It happens to everybody. I do it to myself. I'm getting older now and the shadows are getting longer. When I look into them I see shapes move and stir and I think I remember what they are, but maybe I'm just making it up to suit a reality about myself that I find comfortable.

From January 2005 until December 2014 I hosted a late-night show on American broadcast television. I found it in turns rewarding, frustrating, difficult, easy, immensely satisfying, soul-crushingly dull, hilarious, and depressing.

Sometimes all in one show. Sometimes all in one monologue. Sometimes all in one "interview" (I have never really thought of myself as an interviewer, but if you talk to people on TV and the show title has your name in it then you are, by default, an interviewer, I suppose).

The strict traditional format the show was produced under demanded that each episode begin with a monologue. A late-night tradition dating back to the early ratpacky nicoteeny alcoholic madmen days of TV. My first stumbling attempts were the clumsy reading of jokes written in black ink on giant white cards that were held just off camera by a very nice man called Tony.

Tony's job was holding up jokes for me to read out. It didn't matter to him if the joke was good or bad, clever or stupid. He didn't care, he passed no judgment. He was like a good under-taker, handling each case with professional detachment. He didn't get involved.

I was expected to do the same. Sell the joke and move on, de-liver the monologue. I tried but I was terrible at it, as the early reviews for the show gleefully and wickedly pointed out. I found myself saying mean and bitchy things about people or groups of people who I didn't know anything about. By doing the task as-signed to me, I found myself espousing the rage and questionable morality of whatever writer had been lucky enough to find favor with the producers that day. I found I had to defend myself about jokes I made on TV when I didn't agree or even have much knowl-edge of the stance I had supposedly taken.

I vas just obeying orders.

It became evident to me that if I was to continue on the show, that if I were to espouse any rage and questionable moral judg-ment, it would have to be my own. Otherwise I was inviting a level of self-loathing that even an apostate Scottish Calvinist couldn't survive.

I fired the writers I disagreed with and hired a few whose weltanschauung ran in tandem with or complemented my own. The monologue went from being a necessary chore to being a cre-ative emotional outlet. When it was at its best it was more of an essay that contained the requisite amount of jokes. An op-ed col-umn in a suit and makeup. Not every night, of course. Sometimes, like most people, I simply had nothing to say (hence the annual *Latvian Independence Day* monologue was born). On some nights, though, maybe a dozen or so per year, it all clicked and I made myself and a few others laugh or cry or think about things differently.

The monologue didn't give me total freedom, of course. The concerns of the network or the FCC or the sponsors could be restricting at times. Performing stand-up in a theater or a comedy club with no cameras running is a more liberated vehicle of articulation, but it does require a certain singularity of purpose. It should be funny.

I don't miss doing the late-night show, but my brain has become used to the format of these monologues/essays. So much so that the initial title of this book was going to be *Mono-Logging*. But I thought that it sounded too much like a sophomoric euphemism for masturbation—and maybe that's what's going on here, maybe I'm just pleasing myself.

Herein, then, is a collection of recollections and observations and—occasionally, in the spirit of poetic license—fabrications that don't fit in any other format but this book's. Not really monologues and not really essays, they have no agenda, not even comedic, although I'd like to hope every now and then they raise a chuckle or two. These are stories that I couldn't or wouldn't tell in any other way than the one in which I present them to you now. The timeline is not strictly linear because that's not how I remember things, so you can start reading the book in the middle if you want, but I'd rather you didn't. You'll understand why when you've finished it.

I settled with the title *Riding the Elephant* because it's the name of one of my favorite stories and also because it's a slang phrase employed by potheads to describe being stoned in a foggy and confused way, though I'm not sure there is any other way to be stoned. Foggy and confused is just how I remember things.

It also seems to me that the phrase *riding the elephant* contains a perfect description for a life which seems to take any direction it chooses, paying scant attention to my instructions or commands. The big gray fucker just goes where it wants.

For Megan

But if you study the logistics
And heuristics of the mystics
You will find that their minds rarely move in a line

—BRIAN ENO

Riding the Elephant

1

Riding the Elephant

In the time before I loved you, I never thought of the world as precious. It had value to me only in its sensuality and its ability to satiate my appetites. This was the time when I was ruled by the tyranny of desire. If I couldn't eat it or snort it or own it or drink it or make it cry or laugh or give me money, then it was invisible to me. I had no empathy, but used sentimentality and wit and slurred prose to cloak my ugliness. Even then I was reaching out to find you, almost imperceptible, a daisy on a mountain of shit. Even now when I warm the pool of recollection and look into its depths I can see the ice melt around the old monsters and watch them cast a sleepy eye to the surface on the off chance of an opportunity to attack.

It was a time of a quiescent conscience but not a deep, restful sleep. I thrashed around in the nightmares. In the cold light of day though, or in the neon, I didn't give a fuck. I sang and danced and joked in the spotlights; I drank and snorted in the bars and clubs and made as much bloody noise as I could so I couldn't hear the discordant hymns of purity and constancy that whined incessantly at low volume in the background. This was a time when I would tear the burned flesh of the dead with my canines and drink stolen mother's milk so that riding on the back of a majestic, sad, captured god would not even register as an issue of morality.

I would not be comfortable riding an elephant today, but I was a different man then, and although I do not ask for your forgiveness for who I was, I humbly apologize to the elephant, wherever she may be.

I had been separated from my wife, Anne, for a few months before I attempted my first adult relationship. Her name was Helen and she was an actress. She was English and was older than me and had a cool Mazda RX-7 with pop-up headlights. She wore a perfume called Giorgio that proclaimed proudly that it came from Beverly Hills on its expensive-looking yellow-and-white packaging. Helen had chic Italian clothes with padded shoulders. She had performed Shakespeare in the theater and been on really good television shows and had known Ian Curtis when she was at school. She knew famous people who were still alive too, and she took reasonably priced holidays to exotic places, sometimes with those famous people. She rode horses, for God's sake. She could have groceries in her refrigerator and not eat them all in the same day; she could pay her bills and make appointments on time. I was bewitched by her *functionality*. That's not to say she was boring. On the contrary, she had a great laugh and an unpredictable temper. She was, to all outward appearances, a well-rounded human being, although I question that now given that she chose to be in a relationship with a recently separated unsuccessful alcoholic stand-up comedian eight years her junior. I was telling a lot of lies to myself about who I was then; perhaps she was unfortunate enough to believe some of them too.

Helen wanted to go Sri Lanka. She had read about it in a magazine. She showed me the pictures. Charming jungle scenery and giant golden Buddhas. I didn't care about going to Sri Lanka, but

I didn't want Helen to know I was that provincial so I enthusiastically agreed. Although I could ill afford it, I borrowed some more money from my increasingly concerned bank, and we bought tickets and booked a hotel.

Although Helen had questionable taste in men, she wasn't an idiot; we had separate finances the entire five years we were together. Smart move, I'd say.

The problem with trying to hide active alcoholism from someone you live with is one of balance. You have to drink because you're an alcoholic, but you don't want to appear too drunk because then the poor unfortunate that is supposedly in a relationship with you might insist on you getting help. That's the last fucking thing you want because every drinking alcoholic knows "getting help" means stopping drinking, and that is unthinkable. Keeping your shit together is a tightrope act and is only halfway possible with luck, good timing, and cocaine. Even then it doesn't always work.

Let's be honest, it hardly ever works.

It never works.

The con I was selling Helen on the flight from London to Sri Lanka was that I was drinking iced tonic water, but on an early bathroom trip I had bribed the charming Tamil flight attendant to slip a double vodka into every drink I asked for. Consequently, I slept most of the second half of the journey, and then had to pretend I didn't have a head like a brown dog as we went through customs and immigration into the surrealism of Colombo at night. I suppose if you live in Colombo it's not strange at all, but if you get off a plane having never experienced anything like it before, it is—or was, I haven't been there in nearly thirty years—a sensory overload in the speedball class, that charming if slightly fatal mixture of heroin and cocaine. Literally takes you in two directions at the same time.

The traffic and noise and heat and moisture and smell of the city slammed me the minute I stepped from the airport. The only time I had experienced anything like the climate was in the steam room of one of the health spas that Helen was so fond of. I didn't like the atmosphere of that steam room even when I wasn't wearing jeans and a leather jacket or suffering from a knee-buckling secret vodka headache or experiencing small, fierce taxi drivers yelling at me in a language I didn't understand.

We made a deal and got in a taxi, an old Morris Minor. Every vehicle in Colombo was an old Morris Minor except for the buses, which were giant red double-deckers that had been bought as a job lot from London Transport. They still had the black destination signs on the front and I was thunderstruck to see my local, the thirteen to Stoke Newington, rumble past with at least fifty more passengers than would ever have been permitted in London, even at rush hour on a bank holiday Friday.

We stayed in a big Western hotel in the city that night and the next day I ate a dog.

I didn't mean to eat a dog. Please don't tell our dogs about this. I was hoodwinked by providence and a horrifying mixture of restaurateur opportunism and the excessive desire of bourgeois tourists to not offend.

Helen wanted to see some of the city before we headed down to the resort we would be staying in on the coast. Like the good little yuppies we were, we wanted to experience the local cuisine, but the authenticity which was essential for dinner party anecdotes dictated we couldn't go anywhere that was in a guidebook or a map. This was the last week of the 1980s. There was no Yelp or Internet or even cell phones, really. We organized our lives by Filofax, which was woefully inadequate for on-the-spot restaurant recommendations. After getting lost in a labyrinthine network of satisfyingly cinematic side streets, we eventually settled on a café that had a few local customers sitting at a Formica table playing dominoes. There was a ceiling fan that was moving so slowly it could have been a clock, and a neon sign for a beer I'd never heard of.

A friendly apple-cheeked waiter come to our table and said hello enthusiastically. We said hello and asked for a menu and he said hello again and we asked if he spoke English and he said hello again. It became clear that either he was really keen to get his hello message across or he had reached the extent of his knowledge of the language. In the time-honored tradition of travelers, I pointed at the beer sign and held up two fingers.

He said hello again and went off to fetch our drinks.

While he was away I expressed some reservation about ordering food in this place, but Helen would have none of it. We had to experience it or else what was the point. I said the point might be to avoid dysentery and she called me a racist so I shut up in a huff.

Mr. Hello came back with what I have to admit were two deliciously cold bottled beers, and after we'd had a few each—Helen never questioned my drinking in tropical climates for some reason—my mood lightened and I decided I was in fact being a racist and we should eat. I asked our waiter for a menu and his answer was, predictably I suppose, Hello.

I mimed opening a book and then eating and he mimed opening a book and shook his head, which I assumed to mean "no menus." He then mimed eating and nodded and waggled his elbows in the universal sign for chicken and said, "Bawk."

"Bawk?" I asked.

"Bawk," he confirmed.

"Bawk good?" I asked.

"Hello," he replied.

I said "bawk" again and pointed to myself and mimed eating. He smiled and pointed at Helen.

"Bawk?" he asked.

She shook her head and I gave her a stern look.

"I'm not that hungry. I'll just have some of yours," she said, throwing me under the bus.

We drank some more beers and got chatting to the domino players and were invited to sit for a game. Dominoes being a splendid pastime which requires no one to speak the same language, things were going swimmingly. I had almost forgotten about my food order until it was placed in front of me. A blue willow-pattern plate bearing a dark brown stew on a bed of white rice. I'll never forget it.

That was at a time when I ate chicken. I am, to this day, familiar with the smell and consistency of chicken even when it is diced and smuggled into my presence under a thick blanket of aromatic curry sauce. I know chicken and this, my dear, was not one. Never had been.

"Bawk!" said Mr. Hello, proudly.

I looked at the plate with suspicion. I glanced at Helen, who looked concerned. I looked at the other players, who were smiling at me in the most charming and friendly "go ahead and eat your lovely plate of chicken" way.

"Bawk?" I asked again.

Everybody assured me it was indeed bawk and they all, including Helen at this point, looked excited at the thought of me eating it. I bowed to pressure and took a forkful.

You know when you eat dog. Even if you have never eaten dog before, you know. It somehow tastes like you would think it would, which you probably haven't thought about until now. It tastes a little like how dogshit smells but with curry. There was a lot of spice but it was in there. A four-legged friend.

I looked at the waiter.

"Woof?" I asked.

The domino players and the waiter were horrified. Lots of exclamations and shaking of heads and assurances of bawk. I was skeptical, and when I refused to eat more, an unpleasant tension came into the air. Helen told me I should knock it off and eat more so as not to be rude. I said that it was fucking dog and that if she wanted to be polite *she* could eat it. She told me she wasn't hungry and anyway she would never knowingly eat a dog. I told her I would never knowingly eat a dog either, and she said she couldn't because she was a former Miss East Cheshire Pony Club, as if that had anything to do with it. In the interest of world peace I took a few more disgusting mouthfuls of man's best friend and then made the tummy-rub sign for being full up. Mr. Hello and the Domino Gang seemed to be happy to let it go at that. We paid up and left pretty soon afterward and as we walked away from the café we both pretended not to hear the barking noises and laughing coming from within.

The next day we were driven in a Morris Minor to the coastal resort that we were booked into for a week. Sri Lankan driving may have improved since December 1989, and I hope for the Sri Lankans' sake it has. I also hope they don't have teenage soldiers at checkpoints every ten miles or so either. That was a bit buttock-clenchy too, although clenched buttocks was exactly what I required given the night I had spent on a Lassie-fueled gastrointestinal thrill ride.

I still felt queasy as we pulled up to the gates of the swanky resort. I don't know if the discomfort was left over from my run-in with Scooby Stew or the sickness I have always felt in the presence of third world economics, a feeling I increasingly experience when I'm in Los Angeles. Extreme wealth flaunting itself up against extreme poverty, or you could express it the other way round, I suppose, if you were a heartless asshole.

We drove past a man at the gate who was wearing a threadbare version of what I assumed to be traditional Sri Lankan costume. He was smoking, but took the cigarette from his mouth and waved at us as we drove past. Next to him stood a sad-looking gray Indian elephant. It was large, of course—bigger than the man, bigger than the Morris Minor, bigger than the security gates—but pretty small for an elephant. She (as I later found out) had a decorative headdress on, the type traditionally used on her species by now-defunct cruel circuses. She looked like an old person in a cancer ward who's been dressed up by the nurses for a visitor. It was crushingly sad, or maybe I had a terrible hangover, or maybe both. The man and I locked eyes for a moment and he smiled at me, really smiled. He didn't look sad at all.

"What's that about?" I asked the driver.

"That man will give elephant ride, sir. Not as good as a car. Very slow," he told me, helpfully.

The resort wasn't particularly expensive, but it was in a part of the world where just a few pounds, dollars, or deutsche marks went a long way. I hated it. I felt guilty being there. The view was beautiful, of course. Open lobby facing out onto an impossible azure ocean and a white-sand beach, but the vista was marred by overweight cartoon Westerners sunning themselves and napping like some tropical species of albino walrus. Uniformed security guards kept local beggars from trespassing onto the precious resort sand or approaching the guests.

There was an all-you-can-eat buffet every day for breakfast, lunch, and dinner. Native staff scurried deferentially, the men in white Nehru jackets and the women in traditional dress. I felt as if I were in some super-luxurious open prison for the criminally greedy, which I suppose I was.

You know, I have run all my life. From fights and bars and women and any number of tricky situations. I run to think and I run to not think. I ran even when I was drinking. Often, I would leave bars and run into the night, just keep going until sheer exhaustion or sheer drunkenness stopped me. I don't run in groups or on teams, I don't run in events or with friends. I don't run for charity. I don't run for fitness—I ran even when I was fat or when I smoked. I run for the same thing I have always run for. The solitude and the independence of spirit. The feeling of freedom. When I was in my early teens I read Alan Sillitoe's short story "The Loneliness of the Long-Distance Runner" and had my psyche explained to me.

I took to running down the Sri Lankan beach to escape the horrible Sunday-afternoon feeling of the hotel. I ran barefoot, past the security guards who mumbled dire warnings about my safety. I ran to the edge of the headland and back. It took about an hour and occasionally some local kids would run next to me laughing, until they got bored. One day a young man, maybe in his early twenties, ran with me, keeping in step and saying nothing. At first the atmosphere felt malevolent and I thought I might be in a spot of bother, but we soon fell into a companionable pace and occasionally he or I would speed up to test the other or clear a rock or beached jellyfish in our path. When I reached the halfway point I stopped, as had become my habit, to catch my breath and have a cigarette. I offered him one, which he accepted graciously. We smoked in silence for a few minutes and then he asked me in perfect English:

"What's it like to be rich?"

I sputtered and coughed a little and told him I wasn't rich, which he didn't believe.

"Of course you are rich. You have a nice fat tummy and you wear rich man's clothes."

He had a point about the tummy, but I was wearing a ratty old T-shirt I had been given from the Hackney Empire in London when I'd played a gig there. He wasn't wearing a T-shirt at all. I thought that had been a choice but perhaps not.

"This is a rich man's T-shirt?" I asked.

"Oh yes," he said. "Hackney Empire. Very famous."

"You want this T-shirt?" I asked.

He said that he could never accept such a generous gift, but I could tell he did want it. I took it off and gave it to him.

"You'll have to wash it. It's a bit sweaty."

He laughed like it was a slightly stupid joke and put on the shirt then and there. I have to admit it looked better on him than it did on me. We finished our cigarettes and began the run back down the beach. We ran in step all the way to the resort security guards and then, before they could confront him, he said, "Good-bye, thank you for the cigarette and the shirt."

He ran off in the opposite direction, back the way we had come. I never saw him again. I hope life worked out okay for him. The security guards gave me the stink-eye like I'd broken the rules by fraternizing with the locals.

Because I was miserable and uncomfortable in the hotel, Helen and I quarreled a lot. When I look back, I think we quarreled a lot wherever we were, which I suspect was entirely my fault. She was actually quite a happy and upbeat person; it was I who was miserable. It was never her that I was angry with, not really. It was myself, of course.

Toward the end of the holiday, after one of our regular rows, the subject of which I have long since forgotten, I stormed out of the hotel and stood fuming by the ornate fountain outside reception. One of the security guards watched me suspiciously, as if I were getting ready to make a run for the fence or was dropping the soil from my secret tunnel out the hem of my trousers. I decided to piss him off by strolling outside the front gates and having a cigarette with the elephant man who I'd seen on the first day.

His name was Mr. De Silva. It seemed to me that every Sri Lankan I met had the surname De Silva. I don't know what the story is behind that, but I suspect it is not a good one. Something colonial, probably. Another legacy of the Victorians, those greedy, self-righteous blundering asshats who plundered the world and sowed the seeds of chaos for generations to come.

I offered Mr. De Silva a filter-tipped Benson & Hedges from the silly golden box they were sold in, but he demurred, preferring to roll his own. He asked me if I'd like an elephant ride and I said maybe later, which I could tell disappointed him. I saw that disappointed look on people's faces all the time back then, and I hated it. So I said fuck it, paid the necessary rupees, and climbed up the little stepladder he provided onto the back of the patiently waiting pachyderm. In the interest of clarity and friendliness we should name her. Let's call her Patricia.

We lumbered away from the gates, me riding on Patricia while Mr. De Silva led her down a dirt track into the jungle. The track was wide and clean and was obviously used for vehicles although none were about. Mr. De Silva pointed out some different plants and flowers in a very professional tour-guidey way. Pretty soon we came to a collection of concrete houses and beat-up trailers, which he told me was his village. It was not picturesque guidebook stuff—it looked more like a tropical version of where I grew up—but he clearly possessed a healthy share of civic pride, so in order to be polite I made the requisite noises of awe and wonder as he showed me his friend's pickup truck and his brother-in-law's fish tank, which was outdoors and held no fish or, indeed, water.

A few people came out from their houses and waved shyly to us. They were all dressed quite elegantly, and I remarked on that to Mr. De Silva. He told me this was because it was a special day in the village, and I was very lucky to be there at that time.

There had been a death.

Given his accent and my confusion and the heat and the fact I was sitting on a fucking elephant in the Sri Lankan jungle, I didn't really grasp what he had told me until we stopped in front of one of the concrete houses. He pulled out the little ladder and indicated that I should dismount Patricia.

I stepped down and was led by smiling villagers into a small concrete house where I was introduced to the corpse. He was an ancient, tan-leather-looking gentleman who seemed to be asleep. This was the first time I'd seen death on a human. I'd seen bugs and roadkill rabbits and a couple of tortoises and hamsters that were unfortunate enough to have been pets of a Scottish schoolboy who had a woeful record of animal husbandry, but I'd never seen a dead one of us. I was shocked by how ordinary it looked and felt. The deceased was lying on white sheets and wearing white robes, and the bed was draped in white muslin. There were some candles lit and the room smelled of jasmine or some kind of perfume more exotic than anything I had encountered. I was a little afraid, more from the feeling of ceremony than mortality. Also, I was embarrassed. I felt like I was intruding on something deeply private, although Mr. De Silva was beaming a big smile at me and nodding to the corpse like I should say something. So I said:

"Very nice."

"Thank you, yes. This is my grandfather. We are very happy. He was sick for some time and now things are much better for him."

The metaphysics of this were a little beyond me then, but I'm older now and have been broken down by life a little more. I think I understand what he meant, even though I'm not Hindu and reincarnation seems an unlikely explanation of what happens next—although I've learned enough to not rule anything out.

After a few bows and nods with the cheerful family and elderly upbeat widow, I climbed back on Patricia and was taken back to the big Western hotel behind the iron gates. I tipped Mr. De Silva and, not knowing what else to do, offered him my T-shirt, which he accepted with as much appreciation as if I'd given him a car.

Back at the hotel I felt stoned or shocked or like I'd been on an acid trip or a deep-sea dive—neither of which you return from unchanged. I had seen a dead human for the first time and could not process the experience. I did what I do when I'm scared and confused. I ran away.

I ran barefoot down the beach. There was no one around, no naughty local children, no judgmental security guards, no cool buddy to run with. Just me and the beach. I ran up to the headland as another incandescent tropical sunset was commencing over the Indian Ocean, the dark blues and deep greens of the sea and the sky and the jungle intensifying in breathtaking clarity before succumbing to a clear black night unpolluted by modernity and electrics. A primal, timeless shore.

Out of breath, I sat on the sand and lit a cigarette. I inhaled deeply and stared at its burning tip, which seemed to get brighter as night fell. I thought about cancer and wondered if that was what the old man had died of.

I wondered what I would die of. I was twenty-seven then. I'm fifty-seven now.

I smoked and enjoyed the solitude for a while, then stood up and threw the rest of my coffin nail in the ocean and began running back down the beach. As I approached the hotel I could smell cooking. Greedy Brits and Germans in Hawaiian shirts would be gathering in the hotel lobby in anticipation of the next all-you-can-eat buffet. I was hungry and the aroma of roast pork added an edge to my appetite. It was only when I got a little closer and saw the smoke rising from the jungle that I realized that I had not smelled cooking pig but rather the cremation fire of Mr. De Silva's grandfather. The smoke must have been pulled out to sea by the cooling air. I stopped and felt sick for a moment, revolted by my unintentional cannibalistic tendencies.

It was almost completely dark by then, but the flames were throwing a warm glow toward the sky. This can't be true but now, when I remember the smoke rising from the jungle, I see your face in the dark plumes, your face and the faces of our children. As the sun disappears below the horizon on that strange day, I put my head down and run as fast as I can toward you.

2

Mad Nomad

I was raised artificially in a laboratory. The town of Cumbernauld is a suburb of Glasgow that was designed in the 1950s as a social experiment. The bombing of the city by the Luftwaffe during World War II had not helped the prewar housing shortage, so city planners and politicians came up with an idea to house the overspill population who couldn't cram into the crumbling tenements that remained. They would build a modern wonderland, a cut-price concrete utopia on the farmland about fifteen miles northeast of the city. That way the proles could still get to work at the factories and offices in their unreliable, shitty British cars that were becoming increasingly cheap and available. It wasn't a terrible idea, and I think at its core it was humane, forward thinking. But like the communist impulse from which it was born, it was a spectacular failure in practice.

That's not to say it couldn't have worked under different circumstances, but circumstances were not different, so it didn't.

I've never found the notion that "things would have worked if circumstances had been different" to be particularly helpful. Circumstances are what they are. For example, when British Nazi Sir Oswald Ernald Mosley, sixth baronet of Ancoats and admirer of a certain A. Hitler of Austria, died in the 1970s, the British press (even the left-wing Guard- *ian* newspaper) *concluded in his sympathetic obituaries— sometimes in as many words—that he was a great politician marred by his political leanings. This seems totally absurd to me. What the hell is a politician but his political lean- ings? What they meant was that although he was a world- class dick, he was also a baronet so he should retain a measure of respect. It's horseshit, of course, but a nice illus- tration of circumstances.*

Had he not been born into an aristocratic family, he'd have been hanged.

The desire to provide working people with affordable housing is undoubtedly a decent one, but unfortunately Cumbernauld was designed by people who would never live there. Middle- and upper-class architects who lived in Edinburgh or London in or- nate Victorian structures had the time of their lives drawing up an homage to midcentury optimism that probably looked great on blueprints where it never rains and there's no dogshit or glue sniff- ers. They put flat roofs on the houses. *Flat roofs!* Having a flat roof in Scotland is like living in a rabbit burrow beneath an above- ground swimming pool. It's very, very damp in Cumbernauld. It's still the only place where I've seen indoor slugs. It rains nearly all the time. Flat roofs are for adobe structures in New Mexico, not a blustery swamp that has weather so inclement that even the Roman Empire gave up and went home.

This is true.

Cumbernauld is built almost on top of the farthest northern frontier of the Roman Empire in its entire history. The emperor

Antoninus built a wall and posted a garrison there, but they only lasted twenty years before deciding the hassle was just not worth it. The people were crazy and ungovernable and the weather was terrible. It has changed very little since then. There is also a rumor that Pontius Pilate was born in Cumbernauld, when his father was stationed in the fort on the Antonine Wall, but I suspect that's a fabrication put out there by people like me (maybe just me) to make the town seem more glamorous than it is.

Part of the grand notion of the Cumbernauldian Futureworld was that everyone would have a car, so the roads were made wide to allow these vehicles to travel fast and avoid the congestion in cities like Glasgow and Edinburgh, which had come of age in the era of horse-drawn traffic. This design ethic required pedestrians to keep away from these fast-moving vehicles, so sidewalks were out of the question. Instead there were *footpaths* which weaved in serpentine routes around the freeway system. No crosswalks, only tunnels or bridges, which later would prove marvelously efficient for teenage gangs ambushing each other with sticks and bottles, or even more deadly attacks by solitary and dangerous predators. I still get a jolt of adrenaline if I ever have to walk through a tunnel.

I don't think the town was built to be awful; it just ended up that way. I imagine it like a couple of movies I've made. The script was good enough to get backed and they had a shot and everybody tried their best, but it just didn't work. Like booze and drugs, the design quirks of Cumbernauld nearly killed me, or maybe they made me who I am. I still can't decide. Probably a little of both.

I left home for the first time in 1965, when I was three years old. I'm not entirely sure of the details; my memory of that time period is sketchy even though I hadn't started drinking yet, other than maybe just a wee bit of whisky rubbed on my gums to ease the teething process. The story is that my poor mother, who was heavily pregnant with my sister at the time, was trying to keep up with the domestic demands of the house and was doing the laundry by hand. Wrestling with it. Rinsing it off. Strangling it down to a heavy moist bundle, then hanging it to dry on a clothes horse next to the cooker or the coal fire. On wash days the house reeked of fried lard and my father's smelted underpants. Perhaps that's why I ran away.

My older brother and sister were already in school, so I was the only kid hanging round the house all day getting under her feet. According to family lore, I was a restless and hyperactive child. My youngest son is like that, and my aunt Susan told me I was exactly the same.

"Except you were fat," she added kindly.

So I was an agitated tubby little bastard who got bored watching my mother wash clothes, and one day when her back was turned I just wandered right out the front door.

That's the thing that no one tells you about children—they are irresponsible idiots.

Had we still lived in a tenement building, I would not have gotten farther than a few paces. Life in those buildings was much more communal and I would have been spotted and apprehended by any number of bossy ladies who were engaged in similar tasks to my mother. But everyone was a little more separate now, and there was no one outside because it was raining very hard. The twisted and winding footpaths meant that within twenty or thirty seconds I was out of my mother's field of vision. Conversely—if

circumstances had been different—if we had still lived in a tenement and I had, by some miracle, made it to the street, I could
easily have wandered into traffic.

I actually believe I can remember that day. Of course I could be
fooling myself, but I recall looking at the gray sky and being very
happy and singing at the top of my lungs about being a little teapot who was short and stout. Apparently I had been AWOL for
about thirty minutes when she found me standing on the foot-
bridge over the freeway singing to the cars rushing by underneath. I don't know what exactly I was singing to them, but I
suspect I had continued my free-form diminutive teapot theme. I
was soaked to the skin, wearing the traditional toddler outfit of a
little T-shirt and no pants—a look still popular with out-of-shape
middle-aged men at the Burning Man festival, though it's known
today as "shirt-cocking."

I can hardly stand to imagine the terror of the poor woman
when she noticed I was missing, especially now that I have been
through the traumatic process of dealing with toddlers. Before my
mother died, I apologized many times for what I put her through
that day, although she said I was worse when I was a teenager.

"You were always a wanderer," she told me.

My wanderlust has taken me all over the world, although these
days I tend to wear trousers if I feel like walking in the rain and
singing at cars. Most of my traveling has to do with work. I roam
from town to town and tell jokes. That's been my job for thirty
years, apart from a few side trips into acting and hosting and

writing along the way. Traveling makes me feel good. Or at least it used to.

As my late-night show came to an end, I kind of went to pieces. It's not that I didn't want to leave; I did, but even if I had not, I felt that there was a change in the wind, that the late-night television world was resetting itself and there was no longer a place for someone like me. I didn't know what to do. I thought I might never work again, I imagined *Where Are They Now?* pieces in the tabloids about me declaring bankruptcy or going to jail for crimes committed in desperate financial circumstances. There would be photographs—an old, fat bald man in a badly lit mug shot—and gleeful stories of my demise. Those fears were unfounded: I'm reasonably careful with money, I watch what I eat, and, if I say so myself, I've got lovely hair, but my mind just went to its default position—bracing for disaster. I think it would be fair to say I am a catastrophist. (If that's a word. If it's not, it should be just in case.)

I was given plenty of good advice from people I trusted, many of whom had gone through similar transitions. Sage counsel about not making hasty decisions and giving myself time to take stock and consider what to do next, et cetera. Probably the smartest thing I heard at the time was from my oldest friend, John, who lives in Prescott, Arizona, and seems to have garnered the spiritual wisdom that comes to those who spend too much time at high altitudes. He said: "Don't just do something. Sit there!"

Of course I ignored that and booked a massive stand-up tour. I returned to my old habit of running away, which had stopped working as an effective strategy years before, if it had ever worked at all.

I was utterly wretched. My baby boy Liam was very young at the time and we were terrible at being apart. He would cry and try to reach through the phone to try to hug me when I called. I learned the entire children's book *Curious George*—I can still recite it word for word—in order to tell him his favorite story over the phone at bedtime.

For the first time in my life I did not enjoy being on the road. I began to detest it. During this period I had a conversation with a friend of mine who is a very successful musician. Musical artists are told from the very beginning of their careers that they *must* tour in order to reach their fan base, but my friend no longer plays live. He loathed touring but was told by his representatives that if he went for too long without being out on the road, no one would come and see him if he ever decided to get back to it. My guess is that he was given that advice by the people who had a percentage of his earnings, because you can make more money from someone who is in a constant state of generating revenue, even if it is driving the poor bastard crazy.

That wasn't my story, though. I just panicked and ran.

It's not that I disliked performing live. On the contrary, that was the only fun part of the day. The shows were fine and the audiences were great and I felt comfortable for the ninety or so minutes when I was on stage, but I felt increasingly lonely and bored and isolated and sad and full of self-pity. That's no fun for anyone, but for a sober alky it can be deadly. That time period was one of the closest I have come to taking a drink in over twenty-seven years of abstinence.

I grumped and grumbled through the last dates of that run until finally I reached a point that I had not been to before. One morning I got in the car to go to the airport—yet again—after a few days at home with the family. Megan was standing in the driveway holding Liam, who was four years old at the time. He was very upset that I was leaving, and I really, really hate seeing him upset. Before the car pulled away he motioned for me to roll down the window. When I did he climbed through it and curled up in my lap.

"Daddy, please don't tour anymore," he said through big, honest, salty tears.

"Okay, after I get back from these next few shows, I won't. Until you say it's okay. Okay?"

He said that would work for him, and on the way to the plane I got on the phone and started canceling as many shows as I could without getting sued. What the hell else could I do?

This was a very big deal for me, an enormous change. My financial security, not to mention my entire self-worth, is wrapped up in my ability to do my job. I am also a guilt-riddled renegade Protestant with a dangerously inflamed work ethic. I did not miss one show in ten years of late-night television. Not one. In that time both my parents died, I got married, and my second son was born. I had cold sores and flu bouts and head colds and dental surgery and colonoscopies and biopsies and tattoos. I even did a week of shows with shingles! Shingles, for fuck's sake!

> Shingles is clearly a terrible name for the condition it describes. Shingles sounds happy and sparkly, maybe an upbeat stripper or one of Santa's lesser reindeer—". . . and Donner and Blitzen and Shingles!" As anyone who has had it will tell you, shingles is an agonizing, unbelievably

painful malady. It's like being stabbed by a rusty but invis-
ible dagger multiple times every day. There's a shot avail-
able for it now and I'd strongly advise you to get it unless
you are an anti-vaxxer, in which case you deserve shingles,
you dozy bastard.

When you cancel shows, everybody (except Liam) gets mad at you. Managers, agents, and promoters get huffy, but they don't yell at you because they have been through it many times before and technically they are in your employ. But some of the people who were planning on attending those shows got very angry indeed, and they do not work for me. On the contrary, I work for them and they can be pretty horrible bosses. The majority of people understand that everybody's plans change, that's just part of life, but some of the reactions I got on social media were so vitriolic and hateful that I wondered why the hell these individuals had planned to come and see me in the first place. They clearly hated my guts. Trolls like that on social media are like hecklers or drunk drivers, I think. Most people don't do it, and the ones who do are too dumb to realize or too selfish to care that they are ruining things for everyone else.

Anyway, if you had planned on seeing me and I canceled the gig, I'm sorry. I won't do it again. Liam is older now and has told me that he is fine with my going on tour now, as long as he can come too.

Actually, I think he's considering heading out on the road without me. He is my son, after all. I just hope his childhood is happy enough to keep him from telling jokes for a living. All stand-up comedians—in fact, most people involved in the arts who

I admire—seem to have forged their creativity in some form of childhood trauma, so I suppose I have to thank the soulless modernist town planners of postwar Britain for my life today. Without Cumbernauld I would probably have been happy to settle into a more stable adulthood of quiet desperation rather than the volatile, flamboyant journey I have been on since I can remember.

If circumstances had been different, I would have been a happy kid, which I think would have ultimately made me miserable.

3

Out, Damned Spot

O ne of the more unhelpful yet persistent themes of my adolescence was occasional but spectacular bouts of acne. Given that my skin problems were shared by most of my contemporaries, it would have made sense that everyone would be supportive of each other, but Scottish teenagers are as wickedly thrilled by the perverted tickle of schadenfreude as any Hollywood producer or gossip columnist. I still remember some of my zits forty years later. One in particular—the *Dawn Harrison*, named for reasons which will become clear presently—was sufficiently meaty and revolting not only to distort the weight and balance equation of my face but to alter the entire course of my life. That zit may have sent me into a whirling vortex of alcoholism and despair that took years to escape, or it may have saved me from something worse. Some things we just don't get to know for sure.

Dawn Harrison was just what I was looking for. She was very clever and pretty and blond. She rode horses on the weekends and was kind to everyone and always stood up to the thugs and bullies who roamed the playgrounds and corridors, even—and this still impresses me—if she wasn't the victim at the time. She would place herself in potentially violent confrontations to protect other kids. An astonishing, brave, and rather magnificent young woman. She was from a much wealthier family than anyone else

I knew, and her skin seemed to glow with health and prosperity. She was so far out of my league that I felt nauseated with adrenaline and hope when she smiled at me, which she did from time to time. Then again, she smiled at nearly everybody unless they were bullies or assholes, which I was careful never to be around her. Dawn Harrison made you want to be a better person.

> *Clearly I have a type, because this is also an exact description of my wife, Megan. Right down to the horses and smiling.*

Dawn traveled to school every day from the fancy enclave of Dullatur, which was a genteel Victorian village nestled between green fields and a members-only golf club about five miles away from the shitty damp concrete sprawl of the new town. Dullatur has since been consumed and absorbed by Borg-like urban growth, but in 1975 it was the Hamptons of Cumbernauld. Her family clearly had enough money to send her to a private school, but for some reason—my guess in hindsight would be an ethical choice fueled by well-meaning liberalism—her parents sent her to mine.

I was in love with her from the first assembly, when we all arrived from our small, grubby elementaries to be co-opted into the miserable collective of the comprehensive high school system. In first year (seventh grade) I didn't speak to her at all, but in the summer of 1975 I went to America with my dad, and when I returned to school for the next term I was The Kid Who Had Been to New York. Also, although I hadn't noticed this myself, I had grown six inches in height and apparently leaned out sufficiently to shake the hated nickname "Tubby." My voice had dropped an octave, although occasional words would squeak at a pitch that alerted nearby dogs. I had also developed serious man-eyebrows, which I never really knew I was lacking until they actually grew in. (Sadly, as of the writing of this book my once-manly eyebrows seem to be on the way out. I suspect by the time I'm in my dotage they will be completely gone and I'll look like a surprised turtle.) Halfway through the school year, I was beginning to experience short periods of, well, *confidence* would be too extreme a word, but there were definitely periods of less-than-crippling anxiety.

Dawn started talking to me, and it seemed I was capable of talking back. She asked me about New York and I asked her about horses and we seemed to get along. Much to my chagrin, though, she also got along with David Simpson, who was my friend in class but was to become my bitter rival in the pursuit of Ms. Harrison. He was a nice guy, or at least not a sadistic thug, and those were thin on the ground during my school years, so I couldn't afford to lose him as a comrade. We both knew that we wanted Dawn and understood that our friendship did not mitigate our competition. I believe the phrase *may the best man win* was actually used at some point, which seems credible since that's the way people used to think.

> *It seems to me, particularly in politics, that no one really cares about the best man or woman winning, just the one who they support. Loyalty is not borne so much out of admiration or respect for their candidate, but more out of the hatred of the opponent. "Sure he's a grabby sex pest/pedophile/traitor, but he's our grabby sex pest/pedophile/traitor." This is an inevitable result of slanderous negative campaigning and an ineffective, partisan, and mostly lazy media*

who will cut and paste any old fucking cabbage in order to
be first with the clickbait link. Although let's not forget to
blame the vast majority of people who are sheep and do not
wish to have their beliefs challenged while they roll around
with their pals in their own smug, self-righteous shit.

One day in the school library, Jim Love, the famous fourth-year
(tenth-grade) bad boy, actually head-butted Mr. Biggins, the PE
teacher, when they got into an argument about the correct clothing
for school. The ensuing drama and melee resulted in all the kids
huddling in lockdown among the books while the police raced to
the scene. Violence against teachers was a very, very big taboo. An
absolute planet killer. They were allowed to hit you, but if you hit
them back that was assault, and you were going to jail. It was a
flawed system. I think we all agree on that now.

The happy accident during this drama was that Dawn and I
were stuck at a table at the far end of the room with no one else
around. In a moment of shocking pluck brought on by the apoca-
lyptic feel in the air, I asked Dawn if she would go on a date with
me that weekend. She said yes, which so shocked me that I had to
ask her to repeat the answer three times. I would have tried for a
fourth, but I could tell that the saintly Aphrodite of my adolescence was beginning to lose patience.

I took no joy in seeing the look on David's face when I broke
the news later as we walked home from school. There was hardly
any room for gloating (although I managed to fit in a little), as my
entire being was overflowing with happiness and romantic love.
Well, not my entire being. There was a tingling sensation on the
tip of my nose, which I was trying to ignore.

By 4:30 the following morning, when I got up for my milk delivery round before school, a massive zit—or "plook" as they are known in the common parlance of my people—was threatening beneath the skin on the tip of my nose. It was not yet visible to anyone else. Only I and the plook itself knew of its existence. With the boundless optimism of youth, I headed out the door into the dark Scottish morning, hoping that the cold air and physical activity of the job might somehow banish the lurking monster back to the shadows by the time I returned for breakfast.

These days the idea of delivering milk from the back of a flatbed truck in icy conditions in shitty neighborhoods seems Dickensian. I would absolutely forbid my children from work of this kind and it is probably—justifiably— illegal now, but the truth is I enjoyed the gig and was lucky to have it. A job on "ra mulk" was highly prized among my contemporaries. I remember the solitude of these mornings as some of the most beautiful and evocative moments of my early life. The sunrise in the west of Scotland is incandescent and sometimes—often—it's the only time of the day when it doesn't rain. I and two other teenage boys would jump from the back of the old Bedford lorry driven by a surly dairy farmer called Bob and run up the stairs of the flats—what Americans would recognize as project-style low-income housing—placing fresh glass bottles of milk on doorsteps and clearing the empties that had been placed out the night before. The workforce of Britain needs a hot milky tea and cornflakes to start the day, and we kept the wheels of industry turning. The pay was decent, about eight quid (fifteen bucks) a week and all the milk and bread rolls you could consume, which, after a few days, is surprisingly little even for teenage boys. To this day, most mornings I wake up just after 4 and for a nanosecond I think I have to get up for ra mulk and then am grateful that I don't.

I knew the plook was bad before I got home. I could feel its weight pulling my face forward. Even Bob had mentioned it when he dropped me off at my house just after 8 a.m.

"Yuv goat a plook," he told me, helpfully, in his urbane Falkirk accent. The mere fact that he had spoken at all was an indication of the magnitude of the problem. Bob was not given to personal remarks.

Ignoring the bustle of the kitchen where my brother and sisters were having breakfast, I headed to the bathroom to see what I was dealing with. I have never encountered anything like it to this day. Jim Henson's Creature Shop or Lucas's Industrial Light & Magic would be hard pressed to re-create this pus-filled behemoth. Technically it was one plook, but it had three heads. Three creamy peaks that looked as though they could erupt at any moment. The slopes of this organic mountain were greasy and bloodred. It seemed to pulse or throb. It was as if it had a life force all its own. It was a sentient being. A demon plook visiting this realm to consume and destroy. The Cthulhu Spot. Voodoo Acne. Black magic was upon me.

I knew I must not touch the beast, but I couldn't help myself. My index fingers approached it in the familiar pincer movement and almost before I made contact it burst into a cascade of foul custard, splattering the mirror with its first ejaculation, then oozing like a river of smooth vomit from the end of my nose. Now I was committed; the dam had been broken and I had to see this thing through to the grisly, bitter end. My fingers squeezed tighter and the pressure produced more of the foul lava, mixed now with fresh red blood—runny sunny-side-up egg yolk and ketchup. The pain was excruciating, but I didn't care. It was that fucker or me. My eyes ran with tears as I milked and squeezed and pressured and wrestled until all its revolting innards lay across the bathroom sink, an abstract postcard of hell.

I felt the momentary satisfaction of besting a formidable and hated enemy, but very quickly the remorse set in. I squeezed the giant red stump on the end of my nose to see if somehow that would remove it, but I was just pouring gasoline on the fire. All that I was doing was creating more swelling. I looked in the mirror at the damage and knew that I could not possibly be seen in public like this. I could not go to school. I would become an outcast, ridiculed, rejected, and despised. There was no way Dawn Harrison could see me in this state. It was too early in our relationship. We hadn't even started a relationship. Had we been married fifteen years it would have been too early in our relationship. I could not even be seen by my siblings or my parents. My nose, or what was left of it after the Battle of Poisoned Boil, was three times its normal size and the bright vermilion red otherwise seen only on a baboon's anus. It was an extreme emergency, so I had to do what all resourceful schoolkids do in such situations. Feign diarrhea.

Normally my mother would not have bought such an obvious con to stay off school, but the desperation in my voice sold the swindle, or at least convinced her that I wasn't just faking. She

handed me a glass of water through the door, which I opened
sufficiently to let her see my face.

"What happened?" she whispered, looking at my nose in awe.

"I squeezed a plook and it kind of went bad."

She nodded, now my sympathetic accomplice. She said that I
could take a sick day on account of my "tummy trouble," and after
my family had all left to go to work or school I snuck back to my
bed, where I curled up in despair.

When my mother got home from work that evening, she con-
ferred with me and took a closer look. It seemed that there had
been no reduction in swelling, and that in fact a new loch of pus
was beginning to form beneath the surface. She isolated me from
my siblings to spare my feelings and the next day took some time
off work and marched me to the family doctor. This was a medical-
grade plook.

Dr. Cameron, whom I had known since I was a baby, was a
chain-smoking alcoholic who had seen just about every awful
thing nature could throw at a human being. He was not the most
cheerful of souls, but when I walked into his surgery and removed
the woolen scarf that had been hiding my infirmity, he did something I had never seen him do before. He chuckled.

"Wow," he coughed cheerfully. "It's been a wee while since I've
seen anything that dramatic."

I felt a small sense of compensatory pride as he examined me.
He poked and prodded and wiped and swabbed and eventually
put his cigarette in the overflowing ashtray so that he could write
me a prescription for a new wonder drug that had just become
available for serious acne sufferers. Actinac, it was called.

Actinac came in two separate bottles, a clear fluid and a white viscous sludge which were mixed together and applied to the offending areas before bed. I was hopeful as I went to sleep that night, envisioning the medication pulling and drying and fighting the infection in my face. If it was clear by morning, I would make it back to school for Friday and still be able to arrange the details of my weekend date with Dawn.

Sadly it was not to be. Although I was much improved by morning, my nose was still pulsing and had taken on a weird puce hue from the meds. My mother and I conspired another sick day, and although I was grateful for missing the milk run I fretted that Dawn would forget about me before I saw her on Monday.

I spent the weekend at home recuperating from that ten-pound zit, and though my skin had cleared by Monday thanks to the wonders of 1970s UK socialized medicine, I was anxious when I got to class. It turned out I was right to be.

It seemed that David Simpson, having taken advantage of my absence, had asked Dawn out on a date himself. They had gone out on Saturday night and had a good time, going to the movies to see *Enter the Dragon*—an X-rated film that had a sex scene!—and worst of all they had kissed at the end of the night, which meant they were now boyfriend and girlfriend. I tried to take this news stoically, but I was crushed. My only hope was that their romance would fizzle out as quickly, and then I could make my move. But it never did. They just kept going and going; they were still together when I left school two years later. They got married and after the birth of their first child they came to have a drink with me after a show I'd been performing in Stirling. By that time, I was well into my cups and we all laughed about my old Dawn infatuation (them more than me). But even now, forty years later, I can't help but think, what if? What if I had not gotten that damned spot? What if I had taken Dawn to see the Bruce Lee movie and kissed her? Would I have gotten their life instead of mine? Would David Simpson have ended up taking a long, miserable, hallucinogenic, drunken journey through the eighties, eventually landing in Los Angeles? As it turned out, they later got divorced and his life went into a tailspin, so all's well that ends well. I don't know where he is now, but I hear she runs an equestrian center for disabled children, which sounds about right for the girl I knew.

I believe the plook retired to Palm Springs where it lives quietly on the edge of a golf course.

4

Dulce et Decorum Est

By the time I met my grandmothers Beasie and Jean, they were bent double like beggars under sacks resembling the soldiers of poetry. Even still, they were not weak nor beaten. They were both remarkably strong and vital women who intimidated and comforted me as a child. They were frightening because they clearly were from an era when humans had it harder. Consequently, they were not given to verbal or demonstrative affection. They used food and discipline to express love, and when I was in their charge I felt very safe as long as I was careful to keep any childhood naughtiness in check. No one bested these women. Not the Kaiser or the Nazis or Saturday night drunks. They were both born around the same time, about five years before the outbreak of World War I.

Of course World War I was not called that at the time. That would have been a bleak outlook, even for that sad period. Until World War II, the first conflict was called the Great War because it was believed to be "the war that would end all wars." We can look back at that title now and warm ourselves with smug historical irony, but these poor bastards had to tell themselves all the death and killing was for

something, or else what was the fucking point of even try-
ing to carry on?

Beasie Maguire, my father's mother, was Irish Catholic from potato farmers in Donegal. The story of her early life is lost to me. She never talked much about it, I'm guessing because it was a wee bit traumatic. She came to Scotland as a young girl with the rest of her family with the hope of some kind of improvement in their standard of living. Beasie was not romantic about Ireland; she believed that Glasgow was a much better place for the Irish, and there were many who agreed with her. There were also many who did not.

Jean MacLachlan was a Scottish Protestant whose family had moved to the big city from the Highlands toward the end of the nineteenth century. Her family's change of location was also for economic reasons, and Jean was also unsentimental about the country life. Both of these women had been poor in the city and in the country, and the city was the clear winner.

James Joyce said of sentimentality that it was "unearned emotion," which I imagine is a belief he must have picked up from his Irish mother. It undoubtedly is true, though. When I hear people today saying the latest cat meme or Super Bowl commercial gives them "the feels," I want to vomit and then punch them. It seems that although I think it right and proper that the younger generation have a better world to grow up in than the one I had, I am still capable of resenting them for it. I am grateful that neither of my grandmothers was as myopic and closed-minded as this. Perhaps I'll mellow a little more with age.

I don't agree with James Joyce on everything. Literary ge-
nius he may have been, but he was afraid of thunderstorms
and dogs, which are two of my favorite things. Unless I'm
in an airplane flying through cumulonimbus clouds sitting
next to an idiot socialite with a yappy Chihuahua, which
has actually happened. I remember thinking at the time
about how much trouble Joyce would have had with that
experience, which gave me some comfort. As always, if I
can just somehow try to not be selfish and have sympathy
for someone else's predicament, I feel a little better.

I was much closer with Jean than Beasie as a child because she
was my mother's mother and lived very near to us in Cumbernauld. When I was five years old and started school, my mother
took the opportunity to further her own education to become a
teacher. That meant that every day after my classes I would go to
Jean's house to be fed and looked after until such time as my
mother could pick me up. Jean and I bonded over the years. She
was a large woman but didn't seem fat, more like she was covered
in a muscular exoskeleton, which she draped with cardigans and
floral aprons. She wore fake fur slippers with brown nylon stock-
ings rolled down into ankle bracelets at the end of her corned-beef
calves. She always had a large tin of Quality Street chocolates on
the go, and if I helped her around the house I would occasionally
be gifted one. It is a testament to her outsize and commanding
presence that although my grandfather—James, of course—was
still around, I don't recall him nearly as well. He was already halfway to ghosthood, sitting in an armchair in her parlor hidden like
a spy in a crappy movie behind the *Glasgow Herald*.

I realize now that Jean adored me, but when I was a child I just assumed she hated everybody. She was especially tough on other women, tut-tutting at them when they had the audacity to read the news on television or appear on the cover of knitting patterns. I got the impression she thought all other women, certainly those outside her family or social group, were disreputable in some way. I think she may have had some issues with sex because when I was about eight years old she caught me looking at the ladies' underwear section of her mail-order catalog and was genuinely horrified, shaming me with the admonition that I was a "durrty durrty wee boy!" That probably would have been much more accurate a few years later, but at that point I just knew I liked looking at these women without really understanding why.

> *The attitude that I picked up in my early life, that sex was somehow disgusting and dirty and that only someone revolting would actually experience sexual desire, has messed with me a lot through the years. I now know that this is a perverted puritanism in itself, but when that stuff gets in there early it's very hard to shake and it can manifest in all sorts of distressing paranoia. For example, when the Ashley Madison scandal broke—a website that had been arranging clandestine affairs for married people was hacked and its customers exposed—I went into a panic thinking that I would be named in the scandal even though I had never been on the website. I actually checked on the "Is your husband a cheat?" search engine to see if I was in there, even though it would have been totally impossible. This isn't any kind of actual guilt, this is hardwired shame.*

Whatever Jean's issues were she came by them honestly. Her own childhood had been very difficult. She was the eldest of three children who lost their father, Adam, in the Battle of Passchendaele, in 1917. The connection between Jean and me had a lot to do with her lost father.

Adam MacLachlan has been a looming and important figure in my life as far back as I can remember, even though he was killed forty-five years before I was born. He and his hundreds of thousands of brothers-in-arms who marched away to war and never returned are at the root of a titanic melancholy and despair which is still palpable in Britain today. Not just because of the horrific carnage or the despicable propaganda that they were laying down their lives to end war in the world rather than being abused in the death throes of feudalism in service of a twisted spat between Victoria's children. All of that is true, but on a more personal level, World War I had left the survivors of the conflict—mostly women, children, and old men—with a heartbreak so deep that it lasted for generations. In every village no matter how small, all across the UK, there is a monument, usually in the center of town, with the names of the local men who died in the first and second wars.

Whenever there was a quiet moment between Jean and me, or when one of her old friends came to visit while I was around, the subject of Adam would always come up. My mother and my uncles and aunts used to talk about him too. I was "Adam's double," they always said, which seems strange because he died before most of them were born, but as I got older I could see the resemblance in the few old sepia photographs of him. In my late twenties the similarity was shocking; the pictures looked like I was in his uniform. As I have gotten older, our similarities have waned because he was twenty-seven when he died. Age did not wither him nor the years condemn, although my guess is he would rather they had. He clearly was something of a maverick; before the outbreak of war he was actually in show business, an escapologist in the style of Harry Houdini. He appeared at various music halls and vaudeville houses in Scotland under the moniker "MacLan, The Escapology King!" My mother's little brother, my uncle Ronald, still has his stage handcuffs and straitjacket in the attic of his house in Canada.

As I grew into my teenage years and started to experience some minor trouble with the law—drunkenness and street fights—Jean was someone I would run to when everyone else was angry at me. Although she never approved of my behavior, she didn't seem as hysterical about it as everyone else. She told me her father was as "wild as the heather, just like you," and would feed me plates of fried eggs and chips while I watched the telly with her.

We also talked about David Niven. She had liked him as a movie star and I read his autobiography, *The Moon's a Balloon*, when I was a teenager and it had a profound effect on me. I wanted a life like that, filled with adventure and danger and spectacular affairs with movie actresses. I told Jean as much and she said that she believed that, had he survived, her father would have had a similar life to Niven's. Adam had been a soldier and a performer and could write very well, and he was allegedly more handsome than David Niven. I asked her if she had anything that I could read that Adam had written, and she told me she did. She had his diary from the war. It had been returned to her mother with his other effects in 1917. Just like that, she went to the bureau, pulled out a manila envelope from a drawer, and produced a grubby maroon notebook that contained the personal thoughts of my murdered forefather.

After years of being told that I was the double of Adam MacLachlan, being handed this journal in such a matter-of-fact way was a bit of a shock, but it was nothing compared to the chill I felt when I opened it and saw that it might as well have been written in my handwriting. It was a very odd moment.

After Jean died, the family donated the diary to the Argyll and Sutherland Highlanders regimental museum in Stirling Castle, where it remains to this day.

Corporal MacLachlan could indeed write very well, although he clearly was not concerned with spelling and grammar. Given the circumstances, I don't think he can be judged harshly for that. Nothing I have read about the war has affected me as much as this document. The sheer awfulness and misery of his experiences are tempered with an odd, very British cheerfulness and matter-of-fact style of reporting that makes it all much more human and relatable. I think when people are facing extreme adversity they don't talk in brave profundities like actors in action movies; they tend to try to normalize the situation as much as possible. The scope of the diary is interesting because Adam signed up right away at the outbreak of hostilities, so when he first got to France in 1914 there were still cavalry charges and nineteenth-century-style battles with sabers and cannons. He lived long enough to see the industrialization of the conflict as tanks and trench warfare arrived.

One phrase from the diary still haunts me. He and some comrades are taking shelter in a barn for the night when they are ambushed in a particularly vicious mortar attack. He describes the flares and explosions lighting up the sky and says, "It was as if Hell had lost its lid."

Which of course it had. It has never been reattached.

Adam was injured and sent home twice in the three years he was in the military before his death. I asked Jean why he went back. Hadn't he done his bit by then? She told me that he had to go back, that he felt he'd be deserting his brothers-in-arms to stay away. This baffled me as a kid, but having since talked with combat veterans of other conflicts I think I understand a little better now.

There was immense pressure on young men to be on the front lines. Jean told me a story that was not in the diary. Once, when her father was home on leave recuperating from a shrapnel wound in his arm, he was on a tram in Glasgow with my great-grandmother. He was not in uniform and they were on their way to a rare night out at the theater. Two young women approached and dropped a white feather in Adam's lap, the pre-Twitter public shaming method to call him a coward, which was done often to any young man in public not in uniform. Apparently my great-grandmother informed the young ladies in no uncertain terms how mistaken they were, and the shamefaced accusers left the conveyance before their scheduled stop with a round of applause ringing in their ears from the other passengers, who I suspect by that time were growing very weary of this wicked shit. There is a fair chance, and I am not exaggerating, that every single person on that tram had been bereaved by that point. The next time Adam went to France he never came back. He's still there, in a massive graveyard alongside hundreds of thousands of other young men.

In my life I have often felt a strange implacable guilt, and I think it is somehow related to the tragedy of this most awful war. A war so pitiless it spawned an even more ferocious sequel twenty-one years later. As I grow older the sensation of guilt grows with me, and I believe I am very like Adam. I am also an escapologist of sorts. I escaped my school and a few awful jobs and some terrible bands and two bad marriages and late-night television. My instinct is still to wriggle free even though it's clear that it's not always possible.

A few years back, when I had just begun hosting *The Late Late Show,* I was visited by a member of the Scottish parliament who was conducting a survey on the Scottish Diaspora. I had recently been in trouble with the Scottish press for saying in an interview that I was angry at Scotland for my terrible childhood and that Scotland was not supportive of its own people and that if you wanted to get ahead you had to leave. I also apparently said that Scottish people hated any other Scots who were successful overseas—as if thriving elsewhere were some kind of treason. I am not angry at Scotland and I don't believe that to be true, but I do not deny that I am capable of saying stupid, hurtful, untrue things in an interview. I was especially guilty of that sort of behavior back then because I thought I was hot shit for getting a big-timey American TV show with my own name on it. I promise I am cured of that now.

The divine Bill Murray once observed (I believe in reference to Chevy Chase) that when you first become famous you have a period of about eighteen months to be a dick, and if

you don't get rid of it during that time, then it becomes
permanent.

The chap doing the survey (whose name I have forgotten, so clearly I'm still at least partially a self-absorbed dick) asked why I thought that about Scotland. I think I squirmed a little and tried to backtrack, but he said that he sort of agreed with it. I asked him why and his theory was that because so many young men had marched off in 1914–1918 and never came home again. That it had become ingrained in the consciousness of the nation that when a young man left he would never return. That feeling had, in time, morphed into a rage at being left behind. I don't know if that's true, but I felt the trauma of that conflict as a child and I know many others did too.

A shared memory permeates beyond the mind in odd ways, and it doesn't have to be a global conflict to get through. Smaller battles take their toll. For example, one night, around 1979, I was sitting in the lounge bar of the Spur Hotel in Cumbernauld village sipping a pint of heavy whilst an attractive young Margaret sat on my knee and chatted engagingly about this and that. It was looking like it was going to be a very pleasant evening when suddenly the door swung open and Cal Calhoun, a legendary local tough guy, barged in. Not necessarily a disaster, I thought, right up till the moment that the young lady informed me—a little late in the day, if I'm honest—that she and Mr. Calhoun were affianced. I thought it best to make my escape as quickly and efficiently as possible. Cal managed to get only a couple of punches at me as I bravely scampered away. Unfortunately, one of the blows hit the middle finger of my right hand and broke it so badly that it remains crooked to this day. What is notable about the story is not my cowardice, but the fact that both of my sons have crooked middle fingers on their right hands. That bastard Calhoun hit me so hard it got into my DNA. That's impossible, of course, but it's true.

I don't want my sons to be traumatized by what happened to their father or grandfathers or great-grandfathers, but everyone should know about the lives of those who came before them so that they can figure out why their fingers are bent or why sometimes they feel bone-crushingly sad for no reason that anyone else can see.

5

An Education of Sorts

I f you are ever looking for my virginity, I think I might have lost it in a caravan park sometime during the last two weeks of July 1979. The park is in Filey, a tiny suburb of Scarborough, an ornate and pleasingly Gothic seaside resort in Yorkshire on the northeast coast of England.

I had just turned seventeen years old and had been working as an apprentice electrical engineer at Burroughs Corporation—a huge, now-defunct American computer company that had a factory in my hometown. The rest of my siblings would go on to higher education, but I had bailed myself out of school at the minimum permitted age of sixteen. I hated school, fucking despised it, which is still a source of some bitterness and resentment for me because I should have loved it. I'm made for that kind of thing; sitting down and learning is what I love to do more than just about anything else.

I was a victim of bad timing.

There was an experiment in socialized education when I was going through school. Britain was in its pre-punk, pre-Thatcher, smugly bleak, Kafkaesque, crypto-Soviet phase. This was the time when "Good Old Uncle Joe" Stalin was still cautiously revered by the left wing as "perhaps not a good man but the right man for the job." I suppose if that job was horrendous mass murder and genocide, then they were right. Britain in the 1970s was in black and white, Scotland especially. When I see old news footage of that time, everything seems to be drained of color, which is exactly as I remember it. As far as I am concerned, the sepia tone set in at the start of World War I, almost fifty years before I was born, and didn't even begin to let up until the summer of 1979.

It's all perspective, though, I suppose. I remember one night having a lovely chat with the great Irish writer Frank McCourt in a dressing room at UCLA in Los Angeles. We were there to be part of a Rock Bottom Remainders concert. The Rock Bottom Remainders are a band, or at least a loose affiliation, of authors who like to play music but realize that their musical skills are not quite up to par with their literary ones. There's some pretty big hitters in this outfit, among them Mitch Albom, Stephen King, Dave Barry, Amy Tan, Scott Turow, Matt Groening. It was a good-natured event, fun and relaxed. I was there to play drums on one song—The Troggs' "Wild Thing," which isn't a difficult song to play if you have had a chance to rehearse with the other musicians, but I hadn't and made an arse of it.

Frank was there to sing "Danny Boy" or something. (I suspect that's not true, but it feels right.) I was delighted to be in such esteemed company and honored to sit and blether with Mr. McCourt. He was satisfyingly genial and witty and twinkly as a great Irish writer should be, and inevitably our conversation turned to tall tales from the old countries.

My huffy adolescent complaints seemed churlish next to the horrific tales from his masterpiece Angela's Ashes *and I told him so. He smiled and told me that when he received the key to the city of Dublin for writing that book, there were two groups of people in the crowd outside the city hall that day. One group cheering for his achievement and another, just as large, yelling, " 'Twasn't like that at all!"*

I hated school, not only for the violence from teachers and pupils alike but also for the horribly dispiriting form the educating took. Scottish schools were once the best in the world, and in the years since I attended them, they have made remarkable improvements not only in discipline—teachers are no longer permitted to physically assault students, for starters—but also in teaching methods. When I attended Cumbernauld High School it was at the height of big government interference and, for want of a better term, *collectivization.* The philosophy was that all children were equal and that given equal opportunities they would achieve equal results. That is a humane notion, but it removed actual humanity from the situation and made for some odd and infuriating grading of schoolwork. For example, if I had achieved a score of 95 percent on a test but everyone else achieved 100 percent, then I would be marked with an F because more people had done well. The notion of whether I had understood the material was not part of the equation. I believe in fairness and social justice. I believe that all people have the right to health care and education and a decent life, but growing up in this bureaucratic lunacy has forever tempered my opinion of the Left. I treat them as I treat all of those who are called to politics—with *extreme* suspicion.

So I took the first opportunity to jump from the great ship of state and landed straight into the arms of corporate America. I became an apprentice electronics technician at the factory, which employed about 10 percent of the adult workforce of Cumbernauld. Burroughs made adding machines for banks. Enormous analog affairs about the size of a Welsh dresser that franked the futuristic numbers onto the bottom of checks. To be honest I wasn't quite sure what they were making; I told anyone who asked at the time that we made "big gray machines that got put into offices." I was never really that interested in the work, but I needed a job and selfishly bluffed my way into their employ. I regret this now as a form of theft, but I was a heartless, desperate little shit then and it never crossed my mind that I might be depriving someone who really cared about big gray banking machines an opportunity to get the job of their dreams.

My optimistic American employers sent me to Falkirk Technical College one day a week, where I was supposed to learn about capacitors and resistors and be introduced to the genteel craft of soldering. Instead, for the most part I skived off and got drunk with oiks from even worse towns than my own, shitheel burgs like Skinflats and Bo'ness. (Again, with the changed perspective of time, I suspect if I visited these places now I'd find them charming Brigadoons.)

The technical college was a disaster. I had been raised to expect corporal punishment from educators, so the minute that threat was removed I didn't even pretend to listen, barely showing up for classes. This news would eventually reach my employers, who would wisely decide my future lay elsewhere.

The other four days a week I worked on the factory floor with proper grown-up men who had sideburns and beer bellies and wives that they grumbled about. They brought their lunch—"piece" in the colloquial Scottish dialect—to work every day, and the ingredients would be a large part of the day's discussion. Meat = good, vegetables = bad. They would talk about sport, politics, sex, and nothing else. They had their own cups in the store cupboard that they jealously protected and used for the umpteen tea breaks they had every day. Using another man's cup was as heinous an offense as drinking another man's pint in a pub, a shocking display of bad manners and lack of respect that almost certainly would result in violence.

These men considered themselves urbane and sophisticated and knowledgeable and I believed them, although I would cringe with embarrassment when they wolf-whistled at Big Margaret— all Scottish women were named Margaret until 1979—the secretary from the executive offices. She would click past the production line a few times a day on impossibly shiny black Mary Jane heels, the fat on her feet pushing up in sensual yet repellent little mounds through the gaps in the front of the shoes.

Margaret was a vision of 1970s Scottish male fantasy, and her spectacular aesthetic was a triumphant symphony to the diverse range of products available from the petrochemical industry. Her zaftig, some might even say portly, curves squeezed into her rayon Chanel two-piece knockoff. Her immaculate blond Farrah Fawcett 'do, Aqua-Netted into a shiny Teflon crash helmet, would hardly move as she'd turn and smile or wink at some delusional twerp who thought he could shout his way into the (what I imagined to be) big floral Marks & Spencer underpants encased beneath the hermetically sealed elastic and nylon carapace of her sheer black pantyhose.

She was an astonishingly vivid character, a mash-up of Jessica Rabbit, Shrek, and Dolly Parton. I thought of her as being in her midforties, but looking back she must have been only in her twenties. She looked older because she had that love of excessive cosmetic application that is still rife among young working-class Scottish women. Somewhere behind the tan pancake, panda eyes, and crab-leg lashes lurked an intelligent, profane, and witty mind. Her ability to comedically defend herself from the advances of ridiculous suitors was greatly admired among the workforce. She once told a persistent amorous drunk at a Christmas party that he was like Mickey Mouse pretending to be John Wayne. I swear this drunk was not me, since I was way too young and insignificant to approach her. I would have been terrified to ask her the time of day. Besides, although she was the undisputed sex symbol of the factory among the older gents, she was not Goth-y or punky enough for my taste at the time. Rumor had it she was shagging a policeman from Bishopbriggs. A detective. That's how glamorous she was.

I hated the work in the factory, even though I didn't really do any work. My main task as an apprentice was to listen to older men give me instruction and fetch tools for them when they asked. I resented the subservience of the position. Not that the older men were mean; on the contrary, many of them were interesting and fun, and although it was a macho atmosphere there was very little

in the way of the threatened violence that there had been in school.
These guys were lifers; they didn't want any trouble.

The bosses were treated with caution. Most of them have sunk
into the murk of forgetting, but one was a fascinating gentleman
with the wonderfully poetic Scottish name of Willie MacBeth. He
was a pecky, ginger, freckly, hamsteresque man in his sixties who
wore a white lab coat to signify his seniority and knowledge of big
gray machines. He once candidly told us that he was aware that
Margaret fancied him (a preposterous notion) but he wasn't "gon-
nae do anythin' aboot it, because she was only in it to see what she
could get." The implication was that he was so important, so powerful, that he could somehow attain a promotion for her, never
mind that she worked in a different department. He also insisted
he would never consider any form of sexual congress with Margaret because he couldn't do that to his wife. I imagine that Willie's opportunities to be unfaithful were as rare as a self-aware
Hollywood actor—it happens but not often—but the fact that he
said he would never be unfaithful marked him apart. None of the
other guys believed him and it seemed to irritate them in a sort of
"bros before hos" way. They would present tempting, if unlikely,
scenarios to him in order to test his resolve.

"What if yer wife was away at her mither's hoose and Big
Margrit turned up at yer door in a skimpy bikini?"

"Nope," Willie would say.

"What if yer wife goat a horrible fanny disease and couldnae
shag ye?"

"Nope," he would reply, taking a victory sip from his personal
mug that let everybody know he was the world's greatest grandpa.

I believed Willie, though. He was an unusual spud. He knew

his own mind. He wasn't a follower. He was an individual thinker. He was one of the first people I had encountered who was unthreatened by peer pressure.

Burroughs was where I first came in contact with harder drugs than alcohol. I like to think there is a certain kismet in this. The Great American Junkie William Burroughs was a distant relative of the company founder.

The men who worked on the factory floor were working class and proletarian in their pleasures—sport, alcohol, and fucking— but the company was trying to keep up with giants like IBM and Hewlett-Packard so there were also research and development facilities on site. The Labs. The Labs employed guys with degrees from university. The geeks. The nerds. The hippie gatekeepers to the magical lands of comic books, shitty music, hashish, and LSD. Actually that oversells them quite a bit; it was just two guys, Stuart and Alec, who were older than me and my fellow apprentices. They were both approaching middle age, middle class with decent, well-paid jobs, but they had that odd notion that working-class people were having more fun or were in some way more *authentic*. This is not an uncommon conception in a society that is slightly confused and feels a little guilty about the whole notion of class. In America it takes a similar form when well-heeled white kids culturally appropriate music, fashion, and speech patterns from their less advantaged black counterparts.

Stuart and Alec were an unusual pair. They weren't really friends; their relationship was more like a marriage of convenience for them both. Stuart had access to a wide supply of drugs, not just cannabis but also speed and acid and, every now and then, coke or heroin. This was well before the *Trainspotting* epidemic of Scottish heroin addiction. Alec could get only one drug, hashish, but it remains the most spectacular and powerful hashish that I have ever encountered. Where they got the drugs was a secret that they guarded jealously, even from each other, and with good reason. Drugs were *much* more illegal back then. Even dealing small amounts of hash could get you years of prison time, so it stands to reason that their suppliers must have been serious criminals. This of course added to the mystique and attractiveness and made them both feel dangerous.

They weren't, though. Well, maybe they were dangers to themselves.

Stuart was the chubby only child of disinterested Edinburgh solicitors who had farmed him out to a boarding school since the age of six. He was a sad and awkward soul, and supplying drugs clearly made him feel wanted. It worked. Everybody who wanted drugs pretended to like him. It wasn't even that anyone didn't like him otherwise, it was just that he clearly wanted to be your friend so badly that it made you uncomfortable. I get the same sensation today when strangers put on a bad Scottish accent when they talk to me. It tightens the sphincter and makes me feel sorry for them.

Alec was a different story. As a result of some horrible childhood malady his spine had been twisted and his ability to walk was severely impaired. He fought his disability bravely with a combination of cheerfulness, fortitude, physical determination, and shocking alcoholism. I never once heard, even in extreme drunkenness, an iota of self-pity from him, but he must have been miserable beneath the surface because he seemed to be on the run from a life which, aside from his catastrophic physical disadvantage, seemed idyllic. He was married to a woman who is played in my memory by a young Ali MacGraw, and they had two beautiful daughters. One night as we sat in his crappy little car in the parking lot of the Red Comyn—one of the worst pubs in the world—twisted on a highly potent mixture of hash laced with opium called Nepalese temple ball, I asked him if his wife ever got mad about him getting high and hanging out with us. He said he didn't know. He had never asked her.

I suspect that story doesn't have a great ending, but I don't know it.

I was fired long before the factory was closed down.

Before the inevitable termination of my employment—I lasted almost eighteen months, I think—I got to take a boys' holiday for the Glasgow Fair. The Glasgow Fair isn't really a fair, it's a dream of freedom, or a riotous unwelcome invasion, depending on your point of view and where you live.

Glasgow is an old town; when I was thirteen all the kids in school were given little commemoration mugs to celebrate the city charter dating back to 1175. The town itself is much older even than that, but 1175 is when it received a certificate from whatever pock-faced, syphilitic, chinless aristo was calling himself monarch at the time. Of course, being as old as it is, the town has traditions, ancient traditions, which are very important to its populace. One such is the Glasgow Fair fortnight, the last two weeks in July.

In the Middle Ages this was a renfair-type event held on public land in the center of town, although it was probably a little more disease-y than the renfairs of today and I suspect *ye olde churros* are a more recent invention too. In Victorian times ship-yard workers and factory girls would head to seaside resorts all over the UK to roister and fornicate if they were young, or eat fish and chips and stare at the ocean if they were not. In 1979 the wildly exotic option of cheap package holidays to Spain had be-gun to surface, but that was still financially out of reach for a Burroughs apprentice. However, taking a "lad's holiday" for Fair Fortnight was a rite of passage, so I and three of my fellows did our bit by clubbing together to share a room at a grim, joyless boardinghouse on the northeast coast of England.

I have not taken a British boardinghouse vacation since that fortnight in 1979 and I see no reason to break that run of good fortune. The place we had booked was typical of its type—a mid-terrace nineteenth-century town house in Scarborough, Yorkshire, about three blocks from the pubs and clubs and amusement ar-cades that we had traveled to enjoy. The interior of the house smelled of fairly recently boiled cabbage and Dettol, a popular disinfectant in mental hospitals and men's hairdressers. It was a floral-wallpapered, Dickensian affair run by a steel-haired old lady who looked uncannily like the cartoon myopic Mr. Magoo. She seemed to be barely containing the manic fury raging inside her all the time. Her contempt for her guests was palpable; it em-anated from her like a cheap three-bar electric fire. I don't suppose it helped matters that we were four Scottish teenage boys sharing two double beds and trying not to appear drunk or high when we talked to her.

At first she thought we were gay because of our sleeping ar-rangements, so she charmingly told us we'd be kicked out for any "queer behavior." She wasn't much mollified by the news that we were broke rather than homosexual. She told us if we brought any "brassers" back to the room, she'd kick us out for that too.

She hated us and we hated her right back, but we needed a place to crash and she needed the money, so we tried to coexist for the two weeks we had agreed to. This story was being duplicated by the temporary Glaswegian diaspora all over England at the same time. British people trying to get along and have a good time against terrifying odds and deep, lovingly held prejudices.

I suspect most of these places have been replaced by Airbnbs and boutique hotels which have their own Nespresso machines in the rooms. That's nice, but I pity those who never tried to vacation under the beady eye of a traditional British seaside boardinghouse landlady. They missed a useful lesson in resourcefulness, stealth, and coping with people who are hell-bent on your destruction. Most British seaside resorts are frequented now by the old, who are nostalgic for the days of shit food and shittier attitudes. The younger folks prefer southern Europe with its siren call of good weather, cheap sangria, and herpes contracted from the foam gun at a rave.

The summer of 1979 was a confusing one for music and pop culture. Punk was sort of over and New Wave was sort of in, as well as New Romantics, which seemed to resemble effete singing pirates, as far as I could tell. The Specials and Madness were at the forefront of a sort of ska-punk thing that everyone was into, including me, so at night we went to a big dark club where that music was played by a mustachioed lard-ass DJ who had an accent exactly like the one now used by the actor Kit Harington on the TV show *Game of Thrones*.

"Up nex, 'tis Siouxsie 'n' Banshays wi' 'Appy 'Ouse!"

He'd also play the Sex Pistols and the Clash, and of course Bowie and Iggy so that everyone felt comfortable. I can't remember how it happened, but it was in that club that I met a woman whose name, to my shame, I cannot remember. Let's just call her Doris, which sounds Yorkshire to me.

I recall being on the dance floor, dancing on my own, which was perfectly acceptable at the time. I was drunk but not falling over enough to be kicked out. Somehow Doris and I were dancing together, then somehow we were in the alleyway outside the club. She was about five feet tall but made up for it in weight, and she felt solid to the touch. She was dressed all in black, including a little black porkpie hat. She looked like the World War II naval mines that washed up from time to time on Britain's beaches.

I had fumbled with girls in alleyways before, but it was with girls I knew from school and I had always felt awkward and embarrassed and unsure of what to do. There was a tale among the lads that there were techniques of lovemaking that would drive women into a sexual frenzy. Even if such things did exist, I very much doubted they would have worked on Scottish Protestant girls. Doris was something completely new to me. This girl was hungry. Her hands were all over me, grabbing and *assessing*, like you would with produce at a supermarket. I loved it, but couldn't cope, so I told her what I had heard from Scottish girls a few times before:

"I don't want to do it outside."

After a bit more maladroit, al fresco, sensual wrestling, we agreed that I should visit her tomorrow. Her parents had a caravan in a park in the town of Filey, a short bus ride away. They were going on a coach trip to Newcastle, so the coast would be clear.

I was stone-cold sober as I sat on the bus the following afternoon. I was sweaty and nervous, though not from alcoholic jitters or any kind of drug withdrawal, which were not yet part of my life. I was trembling with anticipation that I was about to have sex, proper shagging for the first time. I wriggled in my seat, my trousers getting increasingly uncomfortable. I tried to regulate my fantasy projection by alternately looking out the window at the cold, flat, gray sea nudging at the shore or at the address and time written on the cardboard from a cigarette packet.

She met me at the bus stop like she said she would. She was wearing the same outfit as the previous evening and was accompanied by a friend whose name, oddly, I do remember. Jackie.

Jackie was a tall, skinny blonde with spectacularly protruding upper front teeth. They even peeped out a little bit when her mouth was closed, though it was open when I met her because she was sharing a bag of chips with Doris. Not potato chips in the American sense. Fries. Big, soggy, hot fries from a fish-and-chip shop wrapped in newspaper and doused in vinegar.

We walked in what I remember to be silence, though surely it couldn't have been, to a small four-berth trailer located deep in the heart of the caravan site. For one dizzying moment I thought I was about to be part of a three-way, but Doris told Jackie to go away for a while and led me inside. She took all her clothes off and lay down on the beige sofa bed in the dining/living area. I tried not to look, but then decided that might be rude, so I looked and then decided that might be creepy. I did not know, as they say in Glasgow, whether to go for a hot pie or a shite. I was flustered. I'd never seen a naked woman in the flesh before. I'd seen photographs but clearly, from what I was looking at now, that was something very different.

When I look back now I feel sad for that young man who had an almost encyclopedic knowledge of drugs, alcohol, and violence but really knew next to nothing about sex.

Doris told me to take off my clothes too. She seemed much less enthusiastic than the previous evening, more pragmatic, like this was a task that needed to be performed so that she could return to Jackie and the big, soggy chips. I did what I was told and stripped down.

She looked at me much the same way she'd been looking at the chips. She told me to lie on top of her and I did. I felt her warm flesh next to mine and, well, for want of a better expression . . . tada! I can't be sure if p even touched v.

I recall hurriedly putting on my clothes and leaving. I apologized for the startling rapidity of the afternoon's events, and although I don't remember what she said, I do remember Doris being very kind to me. She said nice things and even walked me back to the bus stop with Jackie.

I got on the bus and when I turned to wave good-bye I saw Jackie and Doris laughing hysterically.

I burned with shame, but by the time I got back to the other lads I was a legitimate Don Juan who had given that little woman in Filey the thrill ride of her life.

I was a different person when I returned to Scotland. Or at least I tried to be. My colleagues on the production line in the factory seemed sadder and less impressive to me, although I regaled them with the story of the wild and crazy three-way I had been part of in the trailer park in Yorkshire. I was a well-traveled man of the world brimming with sexy confidence. I even sat next to Big Margaret one night in the pub after work. I made her laugh and I bought her a drink. She was still out of my league and we both knew it, but she noticed me and I like to think if I had stayed in Cumbernauld I could have been a contender.

6

Swim Davie

The time I spent in New York City in the early 1980s sometimes plays in my head like an art house movie or, less prosaically, a half-remembered episode of *Starsky & Hutch*. I think my memories have a cinematic quality because I was so familiar with the look of the city from movies and television before I set foot in it. Even today, long since the cruel but regrettably necessary Giuliani-era emasculation of Manhattan street life, I still revel at the absolute theatricality of the town. Corporate Olive Gardening has actually done relatively little (so far) to dim the anarchic beauty of Gotham. The camp, art deco skyscrapers are still there, fighting to keep their heads up among the soulless glass-and-steel lozenges erected by Trumpian fuckwits. Like fabulous old rock stars casting their impressive shadows on the bland shores of the Timberlakes.

The people of New York are still there. Ever changing, ever the same. Each new wave of immigrant is despised and untrusted by the previous one, as it has been since the bead deal for the island itself.

I love the people of New York because they intuitively know, whether they are new to town or fifth-generation Upper East Siders, their role in the giant pageant. New Yorkers, without exception, act like Central Casting extras in movies set in New York City. Sweaty fat guys chewing unlit cigars, wildly costumed Hassidic diamond merchants, smug-looking douchebag stockbrokers in those weird shirts that have collars that are a different color to the rest of the garment, wise-ass kids hustling tourists outside Broadway shows, rich old ladies with yappy little dogs. It is all extremely satisfying, as delicious as the fabulous and revolting smell that comes up from the subway, which I think consists mostly of urine, pizza, and rat.

I love the crumbled tarmac roads spiked here and there by outsize barber polls spewing steam like old-timey lollipop trains. I never really understood the purpose behind the steam pumping out from under New York. Perhaps there's a giant underground men-only club where muscled and mustachioed construction worker types in dirty wifebeaters shovel coal into the city furnaces to fuel the lights of Broadway. Dystopian gay power.

I wasn't in New York for long, I think about eighteen months in total, but certainly well past the six-month limit that had been stamped on my visitor's visa. In my mind I return again and again to this period for inspiration and comfort. I learned so much. Perhaps it was less about the city and more that I was in my early twenties and experiencing a failing marriage and the first real blows of active-drinking alcoholism. Perhaps I would have learned all those lessons wherever I was, but having my memories set against the backdrop of this most astonishing human city at a most evocative period is, well, cool. It was a cool time, even if it wasn't always fun. Actually, what is always fun? Disneyland, I suppose, and that is not cool at all.

I fucking hate Disneyland, and I am delighted to say that,
without my influence, so do my kids. Whenever I go there
I think I am going to have a good time but I end up feeling
dirty and claustrophobic and, if I am dumb enough to eat
anything, sick. Coincidentally exactly the same can be said
of any strip club I've been persuaded to visit.

My first apartment in New York was on the top floor of 334 East
11th Street at the corner of 1st Avenue, above Veniero's Italian bak-
ery, where I tasted my first (and still the best) cannoli. It was a tiny
apartment, even by New York standards. It had a stove and a
shower, no air conditioner, and a shockingly vulgar green shag
carpet. There was enough room for two people if they liked each
other and had only hand luggage. If you sat on the fire escape you
could see the top thirty floors of the Empire State Building. It's still
the best view I've ever had from anywhere I've ever lived. Whenever I was depressed or homesick or in trouble or hungover or
high, which pretty much covers all the time I wasn't at work, I sat
on that fire escape and looked at that building and was grateful to
be there.

The rent was $625 a month, which was affordable as long as I
kept my job as an (illegal) laborer on a construction site in Harlem,
but I could never have paid the one-month security deposit without help from my uncle James.

James Ferguson, my father's younger brother, whom I had visited on Long Island when I was thirteen years old, had by then
moved to Purchase, New York, for his new job taking care of the
country estate of some rich uptown swell. He had a small house

on the property and although he and my aunt Susan had been gracious and thoughtful hosts when I had landed on their doorstep with my wife, Anne, I think he was as relieved as I was when I quickly found a job and an apartment in the city. He loaned me the money for the deposit and because I was a little in awe of and just slightly afraid of him, I paid him back with my first paycheck. I also knew myself pretty well by then. If I hadn't paid him back quickly I might have done to him what a few people have done to me since—not paid him back, avoided him, and finally resented him, blaming him for my own guilt. But thankfully, I took care of it quickly and we remain friends to this day. Obviously he and Susan are older now, as we all are, but they are still a vivacious and active couple. They are fanatical about Scottish country dancing and spend their time wandering the earth teaching people the joys of this most tweedy of martial arts.

Back then, though, James was in his prime. Midforties and a sort of Scottish hybrid of Steve McQueen and Johnny Cash. A cool guy who was tough but never aggressive, emanating the kind of manly air that didn't invite anyone but the most foolish or inebriated to overstep their boundaries. He was what my seven-year-old son would call admiringly "a goddamned American" (I've tried getting him to say "gosh-darned" but he's not an idiot and knows the value and power of language—I can't suppress that).

Although I loved the city life, even I could find it hot and noisy and stifling in the throes of the muggy Manhattan summer. So I was excited when I got a phone call from James one day telling me that a friend of his, a fellow Scottish immigrant, big Davie from Coatbridge, had bought a boat.

"A wee cabin cruiser thing, son. You an' Anne ur tae come oan

up here an' wull take it oot oan the watter." James still sounds
like he just stepped off the boat although he's lived in the US fifty-
plus years.

I was thrilled to accept the invitation, and that weekend we
took the train from Grand Central and James and Susan met us at
the station upstate in the magnificent car he was driving, a converted checker cab painted gunmetal gray. Susan gave us the
skinny on Big Davie as James drove us to the dock. Apparently he
was a self-made man who had hit it big in hardware since coming
to the States around the same time as James. Susan said he was "a
lovely person," which was pretty much how she described everyone, but there were nuances in her tone that were clues to the truth
of the matter. The tone she used to describe Big Davie suggested
that he was a poor soul who was deserving of sympathy.

Big Davie and his wife, whose name I have long since forgotten
so let's call her Margaret, were waiting at the dock for us to arrive.
There was no irony in Big Davie's name; he was a three-hundred-
pounder with a giant red-fleshy face that crowded his mouth with
such pressure that it gave him the signature coy pout of the obese.
He was wearing a white nylon nautical-themed shirt that snuggled the undulations of his torso rolls and accentuated his alarm-
ingly prominent nipples. Added to this were his brightly colored
shorts and brown leather sandals with black woolen socks which
contrasted nicely with the deep-sea-creature paleness of his legs.
He wore a jaunty sailor's cap that was slightly too small but added
a fabulous relaxed panache to his deliciously comical appearance.
He had lovely twinkly eyes and smiled and held out his gorgeous
sweaty paw in welcome. I liked him immediately but could tell
that Susan was right. He was cloaked in that fat-man sadness. In

the movie of this day in my mind he is played by John Candy or Chris Farley. Lovable and funny and fat but somehow desperate and doomed.

His wife, Margaret, was from the Marge Simpson school of long-suffering snack makers, also extremely likable and a little on the chunky side. I felt even more sorry for her. She was wearing a pretty yellow sundress that was probably a little on the young and short side for her, and she'd had her hair styled into the lacquered Kevlar style so beloved by Scottish women of that generation. I remember that the fleshy wobbling of her upper arms—bingo wings, as they are known in Scotland—made me nostalgic for my gran. This was to be a big day for Davie and Margaret, the first voyage on the boat that symbolized their American dream. I can't recall the name of the boat, so let's call that Margaret too. It was the standard cabin cruiser type that can be seen by the thousand in every cove and marina round the world. Nothing particularly fancy, about thirty feet long with a little couch on the stern behind the wheel and a little cabin belowdecks. We happily stowed our supplies of meat and beer, cast off, and puttered out of the marina into Long Island Sound.

It was a high summer East Coast day, beautiful and breezy with just the lightest of chop on the water. Davie was a cautious and proud captain and he, James, and I stayed on the bridge (if you could call it that) while the ladies clambered up to the bows and rolled down the shoulder straps of their dresses, which is the Scottish Protestant equivalent of a topless Brazilian woman wearing a thong. They lay basking in the sun hoping the light would tan their skin instead of just reflecting off it.

James and I were drinking beers like goddamned Americans, but when I offered one to Davie he declined it.

"I can't. Not when I'm in charge of the boat," he said, looking at the open container in my hand the way my dog looks at a ham.

I shrugged and offered him a Coke instead and he took it, cracked it open, and guzzled it down like he'd just returned from a cracker-eating contest in Death Valley.

It felt a little awkward and, with what I would come to recognize as the desperate need to talk brought on by trying to get sober, Davie blurted out that he and Margaret had decided that he was an alcoholic and that this was to be his first day of not drinking.

As an alcoholic who was really just getting started on my own drinking, I was outraged and shocked by his confession. How could he possibly enjoy himself on a lovely day on a lovely boat without having a beer? I was genuinely upset for him, and he didn't seem too happy about the situation himself, but he told me that Margaret had decided this would be the best day for it because he would be distracted and busy in the fresh air.

I started to hate Margaret a little bit.

However, Davie's not drinking was hardly my problem, so I happily threw down beers, and grilled meat on the portable stern stove, trying to avoid his jealous and uncomfortable stares as we chugged along over the waves.

After a while we dropped anchor in the bay of a pretty little island. There was no jetty, but the boat had a little fiberglass dinghy attached so we'd be able to go ashore for a picnic. It was such a nice day that Anne and Susan decided to swim to the shore.

James and I declined to go with them—his cigarette habit was so intense at that point that he couldn't risk being damp for that long, and I hadn't forgotten that *Jaws* was set in Long Island Sound. Davie carefully ferried his prohibitionist wife and her precious cargo of carefully wrapped sandwiches to the beach. The little boat was dangerously low in the water with the combined weight of Davie, his wife, and the grub, so he'd have to return to pick up James and me. I remember feeling so sorry for him as I watched him sweat and fuss around Margaret. Clearly he needed a drink but was terrified of the reaction it would get.

I later learned how that feels. It's not pleasant.

Margaret and the other two ladies waded ashore. Davie turned the little boat around and came back to get us; the prow lifted out of the water as his massive bulk threw the whole craft off balance. He made it back to the main vessel without capsizing and James climbed into the dinghy first, skillfully keeping his cigarette clamped between his lips. He sat up front at the bows and a certain equilibrium was restored.

Everything probably would have been fine if I hadn't got in. But I did.

The combined weight of the three of us must have been north of six hundred pounds, and I'm guessing the little boat was certified for a maximum well below that. We didn't sink, though. Not at first.

There was about a half inch from the water's surface to the lip of the boat's hull and I guess everyone thought that was fine. Davie was a sailor and he was sober, so it must be.

We got about twenty feet from the cabin cruiser before I realized we were sinking. At first denial—"What the fuck!"—then the shock of the water hitting my junk. I looked ahead at James, who was already up to his shoulders and swimming, although his cigarette was still lit and in his mouth, surrounded by a triumphant shit-eating grin.

It was a lovely day, the sea was calm, the water wasn't really that cold, so the whole thing would have been hysterical and fun if Davie hadn't burst out yelling that he couldn't swim.

I had been facing forward but James was looking toward the back of the boat, so I read the trouble we were in on his face before I turned around and saw for myself.

The moment remains as vivid to me now as it did then. The look of utter terror on that poor man's face. It wasn't a face built for fear; it was a face for beer and fun and laughing and life. Maybe sadness, but not fear. Seeing fear on that face was an abomination; it was terrifying, but it was the noise that shocked me more. Davie was wailing like a giant terrified child.

"Help me help me please help me, please God, James, help me! Help me! I'm going to die!"

He cried, a visceral animal wail that alerted the people on the other little pleasure boats that were dotted around the bay.

I had seen enough PSA films to know that it is suicidal to try to assist a drowning person without making sure you can either knock them out or convince them to calm down enough to accept your help and not pull you to a watery grave with them. But even if I had not been taught to keep clear of a panicked drowning man, I think survival instincts would have kept me at a distance anyway.

It was like watching a large wild animal caught in a trap. He kept yelling for James to help him, to save him, that he was going to die, but James was experiencing the same primal emotion that I was. It would have been certain death to approach Davie, I'm convinced of that. I'm surprised and still a little ashamed of the icy calm that came over me then, but I'm indebted beyond measure that my cool uncle was there.

James always sounds unruffled, even when he's shitting his pants. He should have been a test pilot. He kept saying in a loud but calm voice, "Swim Davie, swim Davie, c'mon. Swim."

Davie could hardly hear—he was hysterical and screaming and coughing up water—but James kept on.

"*Swim* Davie, the boat is upturned but it's floating. It's just a bit to your left. *Swim* Davie. *Swim* Davie, *swim*."

And Davie did.

It didn't look like swimming, it looked like he was having a stroke and drowning at the same time, but somehow with James calling "swim Davie" over and over, Big Davie splashed and clattered toward the capsized craft and held on. He made it.

Twenty minutes later we were all back on the big boat. Someone gave the ladies a ride back from the beach and a Coast Guard vessel swung by, having been alerted by those who heard Davie's cries. Once they surmised that Davie had no physical harm, they got on their way, and we all tidied up and headed home, towing the guilty, capsized dinghy in our wake.

It was awkward and quiet on the way back. I think Davie felt that James and I should have grabbed him even though he'd have likely killed us and himself.

Margaret kept quiet when Davie cracked open a beer can and crushed its contents into his mouth. She didn't say anything about his second or third either.

I was very relieved to drive off when we got to shore, and I never saw Davie again. I don't know if he got sober or if he and Margaret stayed together, or even if he kept the boat, but I did learn a few things.

Don't go out on a boat with an alcoholic on his first day sober.

Don't buy a boat unless you can swim.

Don't overload your boat.

And if one of us has to drown, it's you.

7

The Festival

I'm not the first person who was born in Glasgow who has a chip on his shoulder, or a monkey on his back, or a monkey eating chips, or whatever the correct metaphor is for seething with resentment from an early age. Like me, a lot of my contemporaries grew up believing we were victims of the system. That we were good enough to make something of ourselves, but we would be forever held back by the mere fact that we were Glaswegians. It's different now, but back in the neolithic 1980s, Glaswegians were stereotyped by the rest of the UK as loud, obnoxious, aggressive drunks. I resented being put in that pigeonhole, even though I was a loud, obnoxious, aggressive drunk. Like most assholes I was only that way because I felt insecure and angry and embarrassed and afraid. I can still encounter all of these emotions today, but they aren't a constant beating drum, and I have managed to scramble together enough empathy to realize I'm not the only one who feels that way.

I also had a belief in the myth of innate talent, that being born with a skill is better than working hard to develop and nurture your gifts. I'm still not quite sure where this came from, but I still see some traces of it in some Glaswegians of today. It seems paradoxical in a town where hard work is revered, but there is the notion that if you have to be diligent and industrious and persistent at a creative venture, then you must not be very good. In sport too there is a belief that if you have to train too hard you are fundamentally inferior to athletes for whom the prizes come easier. Maybe it's a vestige of centuries of feudalism and Calvinism pedaling the hoary old chestnuts of birthrights and predestination. Whatever it is, it does not help.

I once watched an interview with Jim Baxter, an unbelievably gifted soccer player who, when he was young, was as good as any Beckham or Pelé or Best. The interview was conducted when he was older and he was reminiscing fondly and with glee about how the English and German players used to train and go to bed early whilst the Scots players would be in the pub till all hours, often arriving at the game with hangovers. The implication was that the Scots were so good they didn't need sleep or proper nutrition, for fuck's sake. I suppose this might be true, but the English and German sides win more games so it seems unlikely. I never met Mr. Baxter but I was a fan of his talent. His reputation as a flamboyant, charismatic, wonderful player survives him. He was loved by fans and fellow players alike, but I just wish he had been in possession of better information. He retired from football early at thirty-one years old and died of cancer when he was sixty-one. It seems such a shame.

Jim Baxter is often used as an example of how talented people are self-destructive because their talent is too much for them. I think that's an untruth perpetuated by drunks and junkies to imply that they are artistic and tortured rather than just sick and/or lazy. I have met many untalented people who were self-destructive and many talented people who eat right, get plenty of exercise, and brush their teeth. Jimi Hendrix didn't die of genius; he died of a drug overdose. Janis and Jim and Amy and Hank died of alcoholism, not greatness. Elvis shat himself to death because he was lost to the drugs and the food and the fear. These people were great artists despite their appetite for self-destruction, not because of it. Modigliani was a great artist, but so was Picasso. It's not what you drink that makes you a great painter, it's what you paint.

Given that I was indoctrinated with this negativity and that I was brought up to believe that show business people were weird pervy gypsies with money (that's actually true), it seems unlikely that I would ever have found myself performing stand-up comedy, but I got lucky.

The three biggest factors were punk rock, Billy Connolly, and the Edinburgh Festival.

Punk created an iconoclastic and rebellious environment, which meant anything was possible for the youth, who were expected to push noisily and aggressively against the status quo.

Billy was important because I had been listening to his stand-up albums since I was ten years old. Not only was he funny and dirty and scandalous to my parents' generation (who nevertheless secretly found him hilarious), but he sounded like he could have grown up on the same street as me. Billy changed the game for Glaswegians; he made the rest of the UK less afraid of us. We could be funny now to everyone now, not just to each other.

The Edinburgh Festival, the biggest arts and entertainment festival in the world, which overtakes every theater or bar or makeshift performance area in Scotland's capital city for the month of August every year, was a revelation. Even the streets of the city are crammed with performers during the festival. It launched my career and challenged my prejudices. Glasgow and Edinburgh are like Boston and NYC, or LA and San Francisco, or Springfield and Shelbyville. Two towns that are geographically near each other but culturally and socially very different—or at least they believe they are. They have been rivals for a long, long, long time. Neither one thinks the other is really Scottish. The Edinburgers or Edindonians or Edinbrese or whatever the hell they call themselves think that all people from Glasgow are half Irish, and people from Glasgow think all people from Edinburgh are half English. Like most stereotypes, there's a fragment of truth to that (my father's mother was a Maguire from Donegal), but it's mostly an excuse for distrust and hostility. That's nonsense, of course, but it's not uncommon the world over. Hate thy neighbor.

I was nervous about performing at the Edinburgh Festival for the first time in 1986 for a few reasons:

1. I was new to the game and had very little material.
2. I seemed to get drunk—sometimes very drunk—before I went on stage, even if I really tried not to. I mean I *really* tried.
3. I thought the audiences would be made up of English people. This is not an entirely unreasonable supposition given the massive influx of English performers, talent agents, producers, and just plain tourists that Edinburgh gets at festival time.

English people in the audience were daunting because since I was a child I have been taught to fear and loathe the English. It's an absurd prejudice that quite a few Scots still suffer from. I say *suffer* because I believe that if you are prejudiced you are committing an act of self-robbery which will severely diminish your chance of joy or happiness. Tribalism is not just a curse for those who are victims of its cruel nonsense, but also for the stubborn evolutionary throwbacks who believe that it has validity as a value judgment. That being said, you have to be careful about people from Edinburgh. And the English. And the Irish. And don't get me started on the Welsh. Or the Swiss.

Come to think of it, you have to be careful about people.

I'm not prejudiced, I'm just a misanthropist.

I was wrong about Edinburgh, though. The audiences were great, even though they were half English, and I had the time of my life at that festival. I got that first adrenaline-laced jolt of success and it launched me into my current professional, artistic life with a thrilling force that damn near killed me.

> *Not that I think my life is always professional and artistic. Sometimes it is both, sometimes neither. I like to think my old late-night show was professional and had some artistry, but it depends on who you talk to. It also varies from gig to gig. Indie movies are all artistic, but you have to make a living at something to consider it a profession.* Celebrity Name Game, *the quiz show I hosted, was a professional appointment. I didn't hate doing it and I was pretty good at it—I won two Emmys for it—but I didn't hate being a bartender either, and I was okay at that too. I did it for the*

paycheck and was happy for it. There's no shame in a per-
former performing for money. I don't think Jamie Lee Cur-
tis really loves poop yogurt. Alec Guinness hated Star
Wars *and I don't think Beyoncé sang for Gaddafi because*
she agreed with his policies—actually that's a bad example,
there has to be a limit—but you catch my drift. You just
have to go to work sometimes.

At that first festival in 1986, I performed as a character called
Bing Hitler in a late-night cabaret above a restaurant called the
Café Royal. It was a real show; the audience paid for tickets and
weren't just friends of the band or the DJ or the promoter or me,
which was my usual crowd. The show became so popular that we
sold out every night—it was a very small room—and I got asked
to be on TV and I got an agent and gigs in London. This was a
huge leap for me. By the time the 1987 festival rolled around I was
asked to return to a much bigger venue and share top billing with
a very well-known English comedian who was well on his way to
becoming a big star—Harry Enfield.

Harry is a lovely chap and we got along nicely, so when he
really took off the following year I toured with him as the opening
act, and then I returned to the festival as the headliner in the same
venue we had played together the year before. From then on the
festival became a habit. Every year I'd go and drink and perform.
Each year the drinking got more enthusiastic, until 1992, when I
got sober. I stopped drinking in February of that year, and by
August I still didn't think it was a great idea to be around that
kind of temptation so I sat the festival out, instead shooting a
clumsy, stilted sketch show for BBC Scotland called *2000 Not Out,*

where I tried to mine the millennium for comedy even though it was still eight years away.

*By the time the year 2000 did arrive I was living in Los Angeles. I had just finished shooting a movie—*The Big Tease*—and had become friends with the terrific actor Donal Logue, whom I had worked with in the film. Donal lived at the top of a hill in Hollywood with a perfect view of the sign, and we timed it to be in the air above his pool as the bells chimed at midnight, splashing fully clothed into a new century. We held hands 'cause it felt right and we were baptized in the freezing-cold chlorinated water. I haven't seen Donal for a while, but whenever I do we are instantly friends again. We are brothers, welded together forever by a flippant and exciting moment in time. This happens a lot to people and it's not always as much fun as my friendship with Donal. For example, you can think that you have met the love of your life when actually you've just bumped into someone who talks pretty and wants to have sex with you. What I'm saying is use a condom. Unless it's Donal Logue, then you should be fine.*

The next year, 1993, I returned to Edinburgh and had the time of my life, not doing stand-up but playing the role of the Maniac in *Accidental Death of an Anarchist*, a spectacularly vibrant and political piece by the Italian playwright Dario Fo. It was a perfect part for me at that time, very high energy—all monologues and climbing the rafters—which was kind of who I was then too.

Intense and evangelical as newly sober people often are, I needed an outlet for all that crazy. It worked.

By 1994 I was still full of manic energy and ready to try stand-up again. I took two gigs—playing the part of Oscar Madison in a Scottish adaptation of *The Odd Couple* during the day and then performing a stand-up show at night. Again it worked; both shows were successful and I was starting to believe that I was hot shit. I look back on that with a measure of embarrassment but also with a sense of relief that I escaped relatively unharmed. It has been my experience that the closest I have come to relapsing into my old drunken life has rarely been during periods of adversity or heartbreak, but rather in moments of triumph when I think I'm smarter or cooler or less alcoholic than I am. Take heed, fellow alkies, it's the good times you have to look out for. Luckily I was spotted by a manager scouting for talent that year and whisked off to LA, where I would be restored to the bottom of the heap.

I did not return to Edinburgh for a long time after that. I was working on *The Drew Carey Show* for ABC and we were always filming at that time of year. Then when I moved to late night I was always too busy to go anywhere, so it was not until 2012 that I returned to the festival. That was not to perform but only for one night to get my picture taken and the big splashy premiere of a movie I had worked on, Disney's animated blockbuster classic *Brave*.

I'm going to tell you a secret about that movie but you have to promise not to tell anyone. I don't like it. It is by far the most commercially successful movie I have been involved in. It made over a billion dollars at the box office, it won the Oscar for best animated picture, and it has a list of actors in the cast that anyone would be honored to be included with. Everyone loves that movie and I should too. I was treated well by Disney and paid handsomely. The director was a sweetheart and the crew could not have been nicer. It was a dream gig . . . but I don't like the film.

It's the princess. She bugs me. She's an asshole. She has a conflict with her parents about her life and resorts to slipping her mother a magic potion that turns her into a bear. You can't just go turning people into bears if you disagree with them! I had multiple arguments with my mother and father, but it never occurred to me to even spit in their tea. I don't want my boys thinking they are entitled to slip me some sort of ursine roofie if I'm being critical of their life choices. It's a dreadful message. There, I said it. I feel better that it's out.

"Why do the movie at all?" I hear you ask. "It was all there in the script. If you didn't like it, no one forced you to be in it."

You're absolutely right, of course, and if I had read the whole script instead of just my own lines, then perhaps I would have known I didn't like it, but I didn't, so I'll just shut up about it from now on.

Finally I returned to the Edinburgh Festival as a performer in 2017. I could not refuse to go because I was summoned by royal command. Not by Her Majesty Elizabeth II, who is a general-practitioner-type monarch—face on money, wearing a crown, waving, that kind of thing—and rarely has anything to do with the Edinburgh Festival. My order came from Karen Koren, who is the undisputed queen of Edinburgh Festival producers. Karen is a lovely, big, blond, bossy, clever woman who has become a legend in Edinburgh in the past thirty years. She started the famous Gilded Balloon venue, which has introduced many—far too many, if you want my opinion—gifted young comedians into the atmosphere. She is a champion of live stand-up and a ball-buster of a businesswoman. She booked me into crappy cabaret events when I was starting out in the 1980s and was always very fair and forgiving of my emerging alcoholic tendencies back then. She's funny and nice and she's pals with my little sister. Karen told me it was time and she was right.

She was opening a new theater in a converted church at the end of the famous pub crawl route of Rose Street, the imaginatively titled Rose Theatre. It has three hundred seats, no windows, and no air-conditioning. In other words, it's a perfect festival venue. I told Karen I was too chickenshit to attempt stand-up in Scotland after being away all these years, but I would do my SiriusXM radio show live in front of an audience. By happy coincidence, the broadcast time of the show meant that we would be starting in the theater at 11 p.m. and finishing at 1 a.m., introducing our American drive-time audience to a hammered festival crowd.

It was like old times and I loved it. I *recherche*d my *temps perdu* and found them even better than before. The Scottish audiences were playful and generous and warm and hilarious and I could not have been happier to be working for them again. There were also American and Canadian and even English tourists, and the atmosphere was as lively as I remembered it being in the late eighties. This is probably not true, but it was as lively as I can handle these days. I have resolved to return to the festival as much as I can from now on, as often as they'll have me, not just to perform but to soak in the sheer exuberance of it.

On one of the last days of the festival I got an unexpected jolt of perspective. Megan and our sons and my mother-in-law, Linda, had joined me for a day and we took the boys to see a daytime kids' show that was being staged in a circus tent on the Meadows, one of Edinburgh's many scenic, bucolic parks. The only real way to get around the city at that time of year is to walk, so we trudged up the cobbled Royal Mile by the castle and across the park to the venue. It took a while as the streets were absolutely crammed with performers handing out flyers for their shows or performing little snippets in the hope of igniting interest from a passerby. Like a live movie trailer. The noise and bustle and spectacle of the whole thing was extremely intense and I was struck by the sheer volume of shows that were going on. I saw poster after poster for young stand-up comics who I had not heard of, or for older ones who I hadn't thought about in years. I began to realize, given how many people were in the game, how much of a miracle it was that my own career had taken the direction it had.

I mentioned as much to Megan.

"It's not a miracle. People like you," she told me.

"No, you like me," I said.

"Not all the time," she said.

"I'm no more talented or likable than any of these other guys," I said, gesturing to a poster of a comedian who I remembered as being a big shot back in the eighties but was now playing in a tiny venue late at night and, if the photograph was accurate, had become his own grandfather. "How come I'm not in my fifties playing a tiny venue late at night at the Edinburgh Festival?"

"You are," she reminded me.

Which of course was true.

I realized the reason I felt lucky, the reason that I feel lucky today, has nothing to do with the work or my career or the ups and downs of it. I felt lucky because I was walking through Edinburgh at festival time with the family that I love and some money in my pocket, but most importantly I was grateful. Success doesn't remove the chip-eating monkey from your back and shoulders; gratitude does.

If I had not been so full of self-loathing and fear and insecurity and piss and vinegar when I was a young man, I would never have dreamt of getting on a stage in the first place. Those were the ingredients of my ambition. I'm happy I felt that way then, but I'm happier that I don't feel that way anymore.

8

A Right Song and Dance

U nless you are British, the United Kingdom can seem like a reasonably uncomplicated place. Most Americans believe that England and the UK are synonymous names for the same realm. Incorrect. According to popular legend, the UK is a land mostly populated by snaggle-toothed, tea-drinking loonies who are devoted to Her Majesty the Queen and warm beer. This is only partially true. Like the rest of the developed world, the United Kingdom is a country made up of immigrants, with many cultures, beliefs, and gene pools mashing together over time. It is not even exactly a country at all. It is a kingdom which is *united*, hence the name, under the pretend rule of a hereditary monarch who has no constitutional authority. It is made up of four countries conjoined for their—arguably—common good. The four countries are England, Scotland, Wales, and Northern Ireland (Ulster).

Like most *ménage à quatres*, the party is in turns messy, thrilling, smelly, disgusting, and sometimes very interesting to observe. Not everyone involved is enjoying it, and sometimes one of the participants (currently Scotland) feels a little dirty about getting into bed with the others in the first place. This particular orgy has been going on for so long that the limbs and orifices of the participants have become tangled together in such complicated ways that it is difficult to see where one entity ends and another begins. Nobody is really sure who is actually getting fucked, although everyone thinks it's them.

In other words, Britain is *weird*.

The British are perfectly cognizant of their eccentricity. They imbibe their oddness with their mother's milk, as soon as they start watching television. British children's television, outside of a few avant-garde art installations, is without doubt the strangest thing I have ever observed on a video screen. I was raised on such classics as Bill and Ben, *The Flower Pot Men*—two stringed puppets who lived in plant pots, dressed like Devo, and communicated in an incomprehensible language of their own, which sounded like underwater flatulence. There was also *Clangers*—a family of woolen mice who lived on the moon, had voices like pennywhistles, and were friendly with a giant metal chicken.

Remember it was Britain, of course, that gave the world the Teletubbies. Tinky Winky, Laa-Laa, Dipsy, and Po—four Day-Glo, androgynous, plump extraterrestrials who share a semisubmerged apartment/burrow with a small robot elephant that thinks it's a vacuum cleaner.

One of the more bizarre criticisms of this show occurred in the late 1990s when the Reverend Jerry Falwell, the fiery righty-tighty, claimed to be outraged by the Teletubbies' apparent gay agenda as evidenced by the handbag-carrying Tinky Winky.

I don't really understand what a gay agenda is. Presumably it is trying to encourage "gayness" in others who wouldn't normally be gay if they hadn't had their preschool minds blown by a corpulent, purse-holding fictional alien.

I happened to be a guest on Bill Maher's much-missed television show Politically Incorrect *the night this story broke. As luck would have it, so was the Reverend Falwell. I was able to assure him that many heterosexual Europeans carried handbags and that Tinky Winky was not necessarily gay.*

But Po, the one with the giant red cock on his head, he's definitely gay.

To his credit, I remember Falwell laughing when I said that, and I got the impression from him both backstage and during the show that a lot of what he said was, in common British parlance, "taking the piss." He had something of a glimmer in his eyes, which could have just been the early stages of conjunctivitis, or—and I profoundly wish this to be true—the almost undetectable "tell" of a gifted agent provocateur. We will never know, as the Reverend has shuffled off this mortal coil, but I can at least take solace in the knowledge that what I have just stated will have annoyed almost everyone I know.

Britain then. It's peculiar. They have a lot of strange traditions and ceremonies which seem comical and pointless to an outsider's eye. For example, criminal lawyers wearing curly seventeenth-century wigs and black cloaks, which make them look like depressed emo transvestites. Or indeed the tradition of monarchy itself, that wildly outdated deification of one gene pool which seems to produce attractive, vivacious young people who magically transform into sad, lardy character actors by the time they hit thirty.

I believe the real reason that the Brits love the monarchy is their inherent love of theater and gossip, both of which the royal family provide. The pageantry and ceremony of the religious and military roles played by the queen and her family is nice, especially along with the more relatable but still salacious family tribulations. The fact that Her Majesty is head of the church and the state but her kids can still be assholes is a source of great solace to many of her subjects.

I have noticed that many Americans seem unaware that the queen is head of the Church of England, but that has been the case dating back to Henry the Eighth, who formed an autonomous English Catholicism because he was furious at the pope for not granting him a divorce in order to facilitate his marriage to the clever and ambitious Anne Boleyn—the Kim Kardashian of her day—who was eventually beheaded after being framed for witchcraft. Things are much tamer today, despite what the *Daily Mail* and *TMZ* would have you believe.

The British love for this type of dramatic entertainment coupled with their bloody awful winters make for the singular and magnificent institution of pantomime, which is the most commercially successful form of theater in the world outside of the powerhouse corporate monsters of Broadway and the West End of London.

Every year in almost every town in the UK there is at least one pantomime, and often more. They are nothing like the silent, crypto-French, stripy-shirt "mimes" that seem to lurk in every mall in America between the guy painted silver and Foot Locker. Pantomimes in Britain are not individuals, they are seasonal musical theater productions. Comedy and musical plays of wildly varying quality. Big, rich towns have big, expensive shows and poor, little towns have cheap, little shows, but it's not the size of your panto that counts, it's how much fun it is to be in the audience. They are extremely loose comedic musical adaptations of old (out-of-copyright) stories like *Sleeping Beauty* or *Mother Goose* or some such malarkey with songs stolen from the current charts or from classic playlists. Think *Mamma Mia!* starring the Three Stooges but with everyone's back catalog instead of just ABBA's. Pantomimes are traditional theatrical affairs which are colorful and funny and melodic and relentlessly fucking cheerful. They provide a much-needed night out, a diversion from long, dark winter nights huddled round the television eating deep-fried potato-like wood chippings and drinking sugared alcoholic beverages.

I loved panto when I was a kid for the spectacle and fun and theater of it, and I came to love it for a different reason as I got older. Obviously if there is a show on in every town, that means a big demand for performers. Everybody gets a gig near Christmas. If you are an actor in the UK and you can't get a panto somewhere in December, then you are either really, really bad or really, really unlucky. Actually, given some of the performances I have witnessed (or let's be honest—*given*), it would have to be just the latter. Doing stand-up comedy late at night at the Edinburgh Festival is cool and artsy and doesn't make you any money at all, but pantomime is a real job, where the performers get paid. The festival is like an indie film and panto is like a game show.

You don't have to be a good performer to get into a panto. You just have to be asked.

I'm not being a snob when I say this; it's actually quite an advantage to be shit, especially if you're the villain in the story. That way, the audience doesn't feel bad about drowning out almost every line of your dialogue with boos and jeers, which is a traditional part of the show.

Perhaps the best way to describe panto to the uninitiated is to compare it to a late-night screening of *The Rocky Horror Picture Show*, where the audience who are familiar with what's expected of them will know when to throw rice or hold up their newspapers or yell the requisite comment to the characters' dialogue. It is a fucking blast!

Besides stand-up comedy, which makes absolutely no conceit of a fourth wall, panto is the most connected and most intimate form of theater that I have ever experienced as a performer. As part of an audience, it's routine to be transported by skillful and gifted players, but as an entertainer it is much rarer to feel a visceral connection to the evening's events. You just have too much to do. It's work. But panto, stand-up, and the late-night show never felt like work to me. They are *fun*—although late-night TV meant dealing with television executives backstage, which, to be honest, is a bit of a fucking grind.

Panto is joyful and human and unapologetically regional. Because of that it can be unintentionally racist. It is difficult to be sensitive to other cultures and peoples if you have almost no knowledge or experience of them. This is my way of at least partially excusing the fact that in the 1989 production of *Aladdin* at the Macrobert Arts Centre in Stirling, I found myself playing the part of "Wha When Wong," a comedic "Chinese policeman."

Look, before you get mad at me and call me a racist dickhead, let me just also add that the other Chinese policeman was a guy called Brian from Aberdeen who was even more non-Chinese

than me, if that's possible, and that the role of Aladdin—a teenage
Arab boy who to my knowledge never got into trouble with any
cops from China or anywhere else—was played by an attractive
actress in her thirties from the popular Scottish TV soap *Take the
High Road*. I'm not kidding. In panto, the juvenile male lead is
almost always played by a sexy woman with fabulous legs. This
is one of the things that makes Britain great. Gender roles are
routinely switched in British theater, a habit dating back to when
women were not allowed to perform on stage and continuing on
through *The Rocky Horror Picture Show* and *Priscilla, Queen of the
Desert*. In fact, all of drag culture owes a great deal to the influence
of British pantomime tradition.

Sadly though, the "Chinese" law enforcement officer I was
playing was male. Thankfully there was no insensitive makeup
job to make me appear Asian; I was actually dressed as a London
bobby and I and all the other actors in the cast made no attempt
to alter our Scottish accents. The only deeply insensitive thing was
the name Wha When Wong. I saw nothing wrong with that at the
time. I didn't even think about it.

I loved doing that job. The director was an old Cockney gent
called Dennis Chritchley who had been an apprentice to the legendary music hall comedian Max Miller during World War II and
had performed at the famed Hackney Empire theater during the
blitz. Dennis was my Obi-Wan, patiently inducting me in the way
of the chosen few who know how to accurately shoot seltzer water
into someone else's trousers. He taught me how to correctly react
to a sausage that was trying to escape from a frying pan during a
slapstick cookery sketch when, for some reason, a Chinese policeman and Aladdin's stepmother (?)—yet another man in drag

(!)—Widow Twankee (I know!), had to make a birthday cake for the sultan. It was wildly surreal, but it was the first time I became remotely aware of theatrical tradition, of how comforting it can be as not just entertainment but as ceremony. I really fell in love with performance during that show. Dennis taught me the ancient slapstick skills that had been passed down to him, but more importantly he taught me about connection, that sense of cheeky impudence that I believe is essential for a comedian.

I suppose Catholics and people who are raised in the more flamboyant pageant-y religions are aware of the awesome fun to be had from spectacle from the outset, but I was raised a Scottish Protestant. As far as I could tell, all color and joy were to be avoided lest they lead to sin. Life was black and white and dour and then you died of something respectable like cancer and were put in a box wearing a woolen suit before being buried in a damp hole.

What I'm saying is Sunday school really did a number on me.

Dennis, who was in his late seventies at the time, was the first person I met who was old according to the calendar but still had energy and enthusiasm and a sense of fun. He had not given up. As I get older now I begin to realize how essential this is for quality of life and a chance of happiness. I have watched beloved friends and relatives lapse into that weird predeath state called "retirement," and I reject it for myself. I want to grow old like Dennis and pantomimes. Busy, enthusiastic, noisy, colorful, politically incorrect, and singing.

And, every so often, dressing as a lady.

9

Down Under

If you are paying any attention to this book whatsoever, then you have probably deduced that I have not always been the shining beacon of sanity that I am today. I used to think the alcohol made me crazy, but it seems I can be just as tonto-bonkers without it. My out-to-lunchiness just manifests itself in different ways. What I'm saying is, it wasn't the booze, it was me. To this day I think very odd thoughts and follow strange little self-imposed rules, but they are probably more weird and sad than self-destructive. For example, and I hate to admit this, I don't like to wear black clothes higher up my body than blue clothes because I think that invites calamity in some way. I also don't like blue clothes underneath black clothes in my closet. By telling you this, I feel I have finally let go of the idea of running for any public office. I would never masturbate in the same room as my watch or a telephone because to do so would invite death because the watch = time, masturbation = sin, and the punishment for sin is death, or your time being up. To wank off next to a telephone would surely bring news of the death of a loved one.

In late 2017 when the stories began to surface of sexual predators like Harvey Weinstein and Louis C.K. jerking themselves off in front of their victims, I was genuinely

mystified. How could anyone get any pleasure from that? I
suppose it is a sort of chickenshit sadism that allows the
grubby fuckwit committing the deed to convince himself
that nobody is getting hurt. Maybe I'm not as crazy as I
thought. A bit of self-doubt and lack of body confidence
might go a long way with these assholes.

I realize all my magical thinking about the color of clothes and self-pleasuring etiquette is, to put it clinically, batshit, but now I've been doing it so long I figure, why risk changing? It's habitual, and who knows, maybe I'm right.

I was told as a kid, "Don't waste your time on worry. Most of the things you worry about never happen."

So in order to keep bad things from happening, it would seem to make sense to worry about them as a preventative measure. If you don't worry about things, then they happen.

Before my first plane ride to Australia from London—sixteen hours to Bangkok, then eight hours from Bangkok to Sydney—I spent a week hardly sleeping at night in order to worry about the plane crashing so that it wouldn't. On the actual flight, I kept my fingers double-crossed on both hands for the entire journey. Up-shot was, of course, I didn't get any sleep on the flight and my hands were really fucking sore. But I was alive.

I know.

Anyway, even with all that crap swirling around in my brain, I still was thrilled and excited to finally land in the Lucky Country.

It was 1987, five years before sobriety, but I had followed the advice of a friend who had experience of the journey and es-chewed hooch on the trip to avoid feeling like shit when I arrived, and apart from my aching fingers and mild hallucinations from lack of sleep, I felt great.

The other reason I hadn't had any booze on the plane was that I had heard about Australian drinking, so I felt like I was starving myself in advance of a banquet.

I had been invited to the Melbourne International Comedy Festival to perform stand-up. I would be appearing for two weeks, every night, at a pub called the Prince Patrick. Beforehand I had a day of publicity in Sydney. Some local radio, some newspapers, and an appearance on *a late-night TV show hosted by someone who's name I've forgotten,* but I do remember I was told that apparently he liked to lie under a glass-topped table and watch ladies poop on it. It was the first time I'd heard that story, but I've been told it many times since about various powerful showbiz figures and my guess is either it's not true about any of them or it's a very common pastime and I'm an easily shocked provincial oik. A bumpkin who can't handle a blumpkin.

I was interviewed by a very nice woman on a local radio station who, in the refreshingly open way of Australians, asked me if I would like to go out for dinner with her that evening and maybe go for a walk on the beach. It would have seemed churlish to say no, so I didn't.

When I met her later we decided to get drunk and go swimming before dinner. I said I couldn't be too late because I had an early flight to Melbourne and she said it would probably be smarter just to stay awake until it was time to leave, which seemed a splendid idea. We drank too much beer, then ran across what felt like miles of sand of Bondi Beach and splashed into the dark Pacific. It horrifies me now to think of the amount of nighttime drunken swimming I've done in my life. I wouldn't so much as take a bath in candlelight these days, but I was a wilder version of myself then. After we teased the sharks and each other in the surf, she pointed out the southern constellations in the night sky. We dried off, then went back to the bars and clubs of Bondi to get unsober again. I remember standing in a fantastic, congenial crowded pub at about 1 in the morning when a little puddle of seawater that had been lodged in my ear canal ran out. The water had been heated by my own body temperature, and the sensation of it trickling out is still one of the most delicious physical experiences I have ever had. I will remember that moment until the day I die. To this day whenever I take a swim, it crosses my mind that I might get lucky again.

I was a sorry, sorry boy when I got on the plane the next morning, but a few Bloody Marys and a beer set me right and I was Superman again by the time we touched down in Melbourne.

I was the right person in the right place at the right time for the Melbourne comedy scene in 1987. Like me, it was crazy and drunken and trying to evolve into something a little more respectable.

I caroused with local acts who were part of a thrilling new wave of comedy in Australia. Acts like the Doug Anthony All Stars—a four-man troupe of handsome dudes who wore similar-looking military-style outfits and had a profane and hilarious improvised-feeling show. They looked like Coldplay except they were good and funny and not wankers. No one in the group was called Doug Anthony, which I found confusing, but Australians seemed to love it.

There was Wendy Harmer, a saucy and wickedly fast stand-up

who talked about sex so graphically and honestly and without shame that the miserable but not quite dormant Protestant in me was afraid for her.

There were the Hot Bagels, an all-female Jewish cabaret troupe who wore flashy evening dresses and peacock feathers and sang very dirty show tunes. They seemed tremendously exotic to me and were a particular favorite. I became extremely friendly with one of them.

Also there was one of the best stand-ups I have ever seen in my life, a gentleman by the name of Anthony Morgan. He was part showman, part pirate, part philosopher, and all drinker. Anthony and I bevvied together a few nights, but the truth is I couldn't keep up. Australian alkies make the rest of us look like tourists.

There was Mark Trevorrow, whose character Bob Downe was a wickedly vicious parody of cheesy television personalities like the aforementioned late-night host and coffee-table poop pervert.

There was the laconic and cool Aboriginal comedian Ernie Dingo, who I shared a dressing room with at the Prince Pat. Ernie taught me how to play the didgeridoo on the metal tube of an old-fashioned vacuum cleaner, a skill which I still possess. It is one of the few things I can do that impresses my children and is the reason why we don't have a Dyson.

It was a hectic and vibrant and insane time and the nights I spent performing and roistering there will be forever etched in my memory as some of the most creative, romantic, and hilarious adventures I have ever been lucky enough to be involved in.

The nights were clear and dark and wild, but the days were humid and muggy and gruesome and cruel. There have been many times in my life when my drinking took me down some bleak, fearsome alleys, but that Australian trip still looms large as a particularly gnarly example of what alcoholism can do to your mind. This was the first time I encountered the debilitating terror of withdrawal.

I had experienced a couple of what I had called "panic attacks" over the years that could only be calmed with alcohol, but Melbourne brought it to a whole new level. After a few days of hell-for-leather drinking I stopped sleeping. I'd pass out for a few hours when I stumbled home from the night's activities, but I'd come to early in the morning and need a drink very badly. I tried keeping some beer in the fridge of my digs—a small, cheap rental apartment the promoter had provided for me—but I'd always slurp it down when I got home and then fall asleep without saving some for breakfast or medicine or whatever you want to call it. Alcoholics may be terrible at thinking ahead, but we are terrifically resourceful and dogged in the face of psychosis. I found out which bars in town catered to the men who worked shifts—every town has these bars, either legal or illegal depending on the local laws—so that workers who finish a night shift can get a drink before they go home. In practice, though, they're more often an oasis for those among us who can't make it through the next few hours without taking the edge off. These are not happy places; there are no singing women in peacock feathers. There's no laughter or cabaret, just sad, sorry fuckers trying to quiet the monster within.

I had a dream I was in a bathtub full of whisky. I washed myself in it and drank it and eventually slid down beneath the surface to drown in it. I sat bolt upright on the bed I had somehow crawled into. I was still fully clothed. I was still wearing my shoes, but I had pissed my pants and I was dripping in sweat. I reeked of the whisky from my dream. My heart was pumping and I had a very distressing sensation of not being able to tell where the ends of my hands were. I could see them but I couldn't really feel them. I felt as if I had no jaw or face and had to keep slapping myself. That was as bad as it had ever been. I stumbled to the bathroom and looked at my face in the mirror. My eyes were as bloodshot as a stoned vampire's with hay fever and it looked like my pupils were expanding and contracting very rapidly, although I wasn't sure if that was a hallucination. My hands were shaking and I kept twitching. I did not see any creatures or hear the voices that I have heard other alkies talk about during delirium tremens, but I had a very strong sense that the devil himself was in the room with me.

With a comical vanity I changed into clean clothes; a shower would have been unthinkable and brushing my teeth was very difficult given that I wasn't sure I had a mouth. I headed out the door to the nearest bar.

The great Scottish novelist Robert Louis Stevenson nailed the dilemma and paradox of addiction in the chapter of Dr. Jekyll and Mr. Hyde when he describes a "morning after" for Henry Jekyll. The respectable doctor, having drunk the potion the previous evening, had turned into Mr. Hyde and committed a murder. Having returned to his original form, Jekyll sits remorsefully on a park bench. He decides that he will never drink the potion again and makes a firm resolve to abstain. Almost immediately he notices he is transforming into the evil Mr. Hyde without having taken a sip and realizes that the only hope he has of

returning himself to normalcy is drinking the accursed po-
tion that had set him on this course of madness in the first
place. Events have overtaken him and he is no longer in
control. The potion that drove him to madness is now the
only thing that will keep him sane.

It was around 10 a.m., but already the heat was totally unreasonable and the sunlight was blinding. Thankfully the bar I was
headed to was only two blocks away. I had to hold on to the walls
of the buildings as I walked there in order to ground myself. When
you are this fucked up, gravity seems like only an even bet at best.
I was drenched and red by the time I reached my destination, and
the dark and cool of the air-conditioned hovel felt as welcoming
and sacred as church must feel to penitents who are blessed with
belief.

Australians are a practical people and they don't like their beer
to get warm, so in the summertime they serve it in tiny little
glasses called stubbies. These are woefully inefficient at delivering
large amounts of liquid at breakneck speed, which is what I required that morning. I suppose I could have drunk whisky or
vodka or some other hard liquor which can do the job much faster,
but somewhere in my confused and panicky mind I still believed
my father's well-meaning but wildly erroneous advice: "Stick to
beer, son, and you'll never be an alky."

I really did not want to become an alcoholic because then I'd
have to stop drinking, and I needed to drink or I'd go fucking
insane. You see the problem.

The barmaid, an incongruously chipper young Goth, was kept
busy bringing me stubby after stubby of lager, which I pounded

down as if they were shots. Eventually she took to setting them up three at a time, and that allowed her some time to attend to her other customers. After a dozen or more drinks, I felt better and the devil inside began to feel sleepy, allowing me to take a breath. The barmaid seemed to notice my change in demeanor and my slowed pace and we began to chat. She had heard my accent and asked about Scotland and I started giving her the old pickup blarney that was my default position in conversations with women at that time.

"Can I tell you something?" she asked me.

I said she could.

"You drink too much."

I told her that it had been pointed out before.

"Yeah, I'm sure people have said it before, but I am an Australian barmaid that works in a pub that's open in the morning in a shitty part of Melbourne. If I notice you drink too much, you really must drink too much."

"You think I'm an alky?" I asked her.

"Everyone in here is an alky, Bruce. It's ten a.m. But you're the alkiest alky I've ever seen. You're like an alky from a movie or something."

I laughed and ordered another drink and bought one for her too. We clinked glasses and toasted my exceptional nature.

For a while I thought of this experience as a particularly low point in my life but with time, yet again, my perspective has changed. This was the first little sliver of light. Someone had told me exactly who I was. And whether it was because I was vulnerable enough or drunk enough or she was cute enough or the information was presented without judgment or criticism, I heard it. I believed it.

It was five years later when I finally stumbled into sobriety, and all through that time I was haunted by that conversation. I wasn't exceptional, of course. I was just the same as any other poor twitching bugger in any bar at 10 a.m. trying to stop their heart from bursting through their chest, but somewhere in that exchange I had begun to hear a message. A seed began to grow, a notion that I was a drunk who couldn't stop drinking. There's a name for people like that. The fact that I was beginning to understand who and what I was constituted a victory of sorts. It was a turning point in the war that I was losing badly. If I may paraphrase another boozehound who was much better at winning much bigger wars—*this was not the end. It was not even the beginning of the end, but it was, perhaps, the end of the beginning.*

10

The Helpers

No topic, it seems, fires up people more than religion. It inspires the good and the wicked alike. Finding some omnipotent celestial vicar to endorse whatever cruelty or oppression you want to impose on others has always been a great tool for the evil—a point much repeated by atheists who, quite religiously, like to jeer at and condemn anyone who disagrees with them. Of course, there have been countless good and noble deeds performed in the name of (*insert deity of your choice here*), but I always suspected the perpetrators of both good and evil probably would have behaved the same way, God or no God.

Most of the time, when religion is used as a motive it is really just an excuse.

To me, it's like a sailing club. I like sailing, I like the ocean, I enjoy wearing stripy T-shirts and a jaunty captain's hat. I'll even hum along with Jimmy Buffett's "Margaritaville" if it comes on the radio when I'm driving. But I'm not so crazy about sailing that I want to join a club. If you do, that's fine with me, and you, as a member of the club, should be cool with me not joining. Why would you want me anyway? I'm not as into it as you are. I'd be faking it.

Most people in the club feel this way, but not everyone. There's always some cunt who wants the whole world to wear espadrilles and a life jacket. Well, fuck that guy.

The temptation with religion is to mock it, and there is certainly much to mock in the absurd ceremonies and camp hijinks of most of the great world religions. From the ceremonial cannibalism of the Jesus wine-and-biscuit snacking to the ludicrous pseudoscience of the E-meter, from the magical Mormon underwear to the *GuyWhoseNameYouCan'tEvenSay* (not Voldemort).

I believe that religion is actually a neutral force. Like any other neutral force, from time to nuclear physics, the user is the one who determines whether the outcome is good or bad. Nuclear physics can power your city or lay waste to it; the atoms that are splitting have no moral compass, they don't care whether they create or destroy. They are just doing what *you* set in motion according to the laws of physics. Time passes, whether you spend it wisely or squander it. The minutes themselves cast no judgment on your behavior. In other words, time and nuclear physics just don't give a shit about you and your problems. Perhaps religion is the same way. It doesn't really give a shit about you or your problems, it just does what you make it do.

The modern discussion of religion seems to be dominated by two questions: whether there is a God, and whether there is a continuation of consciousness after death. To me these are separate issues that have become welded together. The reason for this is not due to chance or ignorance; it contains a malevolence which is as old as our species.

Power.

In much the same way that many people believe that

capitalism is somehow synonymous with democracy, many people believe that religion is about God. The reason they have become welded together and sold as a job lot to the populace/proles/peasants/the people/us, is that religion, like capitalism, tends to serve some people whilst exploiting others.

It is a tool.

If I can fool you into believing that membership in my particular group will guarantee you immortality and peace and contentment for you and your loved ones for all eternity, then it gives me a fabulous amount of power over you. If I am a good person, I use that power to manipulate you into altruistic and social behavior. If I am a fucking jackass, as so many prominent religious figures have been and continue to be, then I use that power to get you to hand me all your cash and blow me.

As we can observe from politics, the acquisition of power tends to draw the worst people in our species. The narcissistic, sniveling demagogues who are so insecure about themselves and their ideas that they have to oppress all discussion and dissent, whether by force or by decrying any contrary opinion as treason or lunacy. It attracts them as flies to shit. That's why the Enlightenment was so . . . well, enlightening. Enlightenment thought doesn't say there is no God; Enlightenment thought claims that God doesn't make kings, we do.

God doesn't choose the leaders. If there is a God, more than likely She (I'd tend to imagine a benevolent creator in the feminine) sees who we put in charge and it strains Her unconditional love for us.

There are exceptions to this, of course; some political and religious leaders really are good and kind people who care deeply about their fellow humans. There's (*insert politician of choice here*) and then there's (*insert religious figure of choice here*).

The use of religion as a way for contemporary American politicians to curry favor with religious people is not only shameful but contrary to the spirit of the American experiment. Whenever there is a national tragedy, both right-wing and left-wing politicians are always bleating about their "thoughts and prayers," but I have a hard time believing that any of them have a thought or prayer for anything other than their own advancement.

Why is it any more ennobling for someone to claim to be a person of faith rather than a person of doubt? I *like* people of doubt. I like people who question what the hell is going on. St. Thomas is my favorite apostle, even if he was wrong. Galileo smelled a rat, and he was right. It doesn't matter what you believe; it only matters how you behave. Or as it so succinctly says in Christian scripture, "Faith without works is dead." Believe what you like, but this is what I believe. God, if there is one, speaks and expresses Herself through a group of people who the great becardiganed philosopher Fred Rogers called "helpers."

> *The idea of a benevolent, omnipotent God was logically trounced by William of Ockham in the thirteenth century when he stated that (basically) if God is all good, then evil cannot exist. But since evil clearly does exist, God is either not all good or not omnipotent. *mic drop**

Helpers are people who try to make life more bearable for those who are suffering. They are people who try to clean up the mess, are tolerant of the weak-minded, and resist those who would exploit others for their pleasure or profit. A few years ago the UK was plagued by street riots, thousands of mostly young people in hoodies who connected via Twitter and took to the streets in an orgy of violence, vandalism, and looting that was borne more from urban ennui than any identifiable polemic. It was shocking and frightening for the majority of the population, and it took law enforcement quite a while to restore order, but when they inevitably did and the streets were cleared, an inspiring spiritual phenomenon occurred. These same streets, which days before had been filled with aggressive nihilists, became packed with even larger crowds who held their brooms in the air as a gesture of defiance against the madness, before sweeping up the mess and broken glass left in its wake.

These people were helpers. They were young and old, gay and straight, Christian, Muslim, Jew, and Hindu, believers and *un*believers. Some were probably even repentant rioters.

They were helping. This to me is an expression of the divine.

I have benefited from helpers on a more personal level too. In 1991 I was coming to the end of what I hoped was my last drunk. I don't know if I drifted into alcoholism or was born with it, but by the time I was twenty-nine, which I was then, it didn't really matter. It was obvious that I was an alcoholic, and I seemed to be beyond the help of the people who cared for me or of even helping myself. Those who have been ravaged by the perplexing malaise of alcoholism are familiar with this condition. It is despairing.

My girlfriend, Helen, was at her wit's end with my sad drunken disappearances and subsequent remorse. She had found, near the front of the telephone directory, the number of an organization that reportedly helped drunks.

Under protest I attended one of their meetings, not because I thought they could do anything for me, but because I thought it might placate the woman I was supposed to be in a relationship with. I have a dim memory of that meeting, but I do remember Tommy. He was my first helper.

Tommy was from Liverpool. He was older than me and had palled around with the Beatles in the sixties and lived a big, high, drunken, selfish life until crashing and burning disastrously in the eighties. He told me about himself, honestly and without making any moral judgment. Without asking me to believe in anything that he believed and *without preaching*, he explained to me that in order for me to escape the vicious cycle I was in, I would probably have to do what he had done. I had to stop drinking and develop a different attitude about myself and the world around me. Or to put it another way, I had to change my behavior in order to change the way I felt. Action creates thought, not the other way round. Not the rather grand Descartian proclamation "I think, therefore I am," but rather a more pragmatic philosophy of "I am, therefore I think."

I didn't stop drinking that night or even that year, but I couldn't forget Tommy or our brief conversation. It would haunt me as I was talking shite in bars or trying to lie my way out of trouble. It added to the stark message I had received from the Australian barmaid. My problem wasn't that I was a poetically troubled artist. My problem was that once I started drinking alcohol I seemed to be incapable of stopping. In order to change my life, I had to not have *the first drink*, which was the only one I seemed to have any choice about taking.

Eventually, after I got sober, Tommy became a friend. He

planted in me the idea that redemption comes not through some theoretical wishful thinking but through behavior.

He used to say, "If you want to do something spiritual, clean up after the meeting," but since he was also reassuringly realistic, he'd also say, "It's much easier to feel spiritual with a few bob in your pocket."

He didn't ask me to be divine. Just to help out. The rest would take care of itself. He was teaching me to be a helper.

So if I have a religion it's in appreciation of helpers, whoever they happen to be at the time. I've tried not believing in God, but that's just as hard as swallowing all of the liturgical mumbo jumbo. I don't know who or what composed our universe, but I'm not sure that matters anyway. I suspect that any real spiritual peace lies in simply being a decent human being. Or at least trying to be.

11

Four Queens

The moment I touched her hand I knew she was going to die. I knew she knew it too. Her name was Alison but to me she was an Eve, the end of my innocence. We only talked for a little while at a party almost forty years ago, so it would be absurd to say we were close, but I have thought about her many times over the years. She was only sixteen and I remember her as beautiful and sad and clever. I don't know if she was like that all the time, but she definitely was for about a half an hour in 1979.

I was seventeen when I met her at a party at Gillian's house. Gillian was a cantankerous, sexy young woman who I wanted to be my girlfriend. I had experienced a rudimentary ramshackle introduction to the mechanics of sex from that zaftig and exotic—to me anyway—Yorkshire-puddingista on my recent holiday with the lads from work, and I was ready for more practice in that sort of thing. Although Gillian was grumpy, she had a great laugh and thought I was funny. Back then, that was more than enough reason to love her. I was desperate to be in love, to say "I love you" to a girl when I wasn't drunk and she wasn't imaginary.

I suspected that Gillian fancied me too and that that was one of the reasons she'd had the party. That way she could invite me to her house without leaving herself open to rejection. If I came, I came; if I didn't, I didn't. But I did.

Teenage parties are awkward no matter what, but this one was even more uncomfortable than most, since many of the kids at the party had gone to different schools and were very leery of each other. Some kids were Catholic and some were Protestant and we had all been raised to treat the other side with, at best, caution and, at worst, hostility and violence. An uneasy truce hung in the air that night; none of the real headbangers from either faction were in attendance, so it was possible to pursue the much more alluring though equally perilous pastime of teenage courtship.

Gillian was playing grown-up hostess and steered me through the room introducing me to guests I didn't know who came from across the sectarian divide. Eventually we got to Alison, a very pale girl with the telltale chemo do-rag on her head. The only other person I had ever seen who had cancer was my grandfather, who had died the previous year. His appearance had shocked me less because he was old and I was young. Old people are from a different tribe than the young. The young are in firm denial of their own mortality. That's why they can be talked into being kamikaze pilots or suicide bombers, or take shocking risks with their own personal safety through stupid stunts and excessive alcohol and drugs. The idea of *not being* is incomprehensible to them.

Alison was holding court with a couple of chubby and hostile (to me, anyway) teenage girls. Nasty little drama vampires feeding greedily from her tragedy. Gillian introduced us.

At the time, I felt like I was being put through some kind of test. I thought that Gillian wanted to see how I would react to Alison, but later she told me that she actually wanted to see how Alison reacted to me. Get her opinion of a potential suitor. Gillian drifted off, taking the unpleasant supporting players with her.

Alison and I shook hands and she apologized for her hand-shake being limp.

"I've got cancer," she said, "and the chemotherapy makes me feel weak."

A thought flashed that I shouldn't touch her, lest I somehow be infected. I immediately felt ashamed and she smiled at me, as if reading my mind.

"It's not catching," she said.

"How did you get it?" I asked.

"I don't know, nobody knows."

"Well, I'm sure you'll get better," I said clumsily.

"Thanks, Doctor," she said. "But I think you're wrong."

"Are you going to die?" I asked.

She nodded.

"When?" I said.

"I've got about six months, I think."

"That's terrible," I said, and then, for no reason I can think of, I said, "Are you okay?"

She laughed.

"No. I'm dying."

"I'm sorry. I don't know why I said that. It was stupid. I don't know what to say."

She told me it was okay, that people said that to her all the time. It seemed that they wanted to be reassured that she wasn't pan-icky or upset, that she wouldn't make a scene, I suppose.

I apologized again and she changed the subject. She asked me if I fancied Gillian and I said I did and she told me that Gillian fancied me, which was great news. We started talking about mu-sic. She liked Stevie Wonder, which was very odd to me. I'd heard of him, of course, and heard his music, but in the west of Scotland in the late 1970s nobody I knew listened to that. We were punks or mods or (God help us) New Romantics.

We talked about fashion and football and religion and sectarianism. And since I was a selfish teenage boy, we talked about me a lot. My favorite subject at the time. Less so now, in the same way I no longer enjoy looking at my reflection. One of the gifts of age, I suppose.

Old age was a gift Alison never got. I never saw her again. She died almost a year later. Gillian and I were thinking about getting engaged, but we never did. We made the choice to move on in different directions, but Alison didn't move on; she stopped right there in that shitty town. Her ghost floats next to my mother and my father in a packed little graveyard guarded by the unkindness of ravens who inhabit the old, tall pines on its border.

At first, and for a few years afterward, I didn't think of Alison much. I was sorry for her and sorry for her family, of course, and I felt the terrible sadness of it. But as time has passed I think of her more, because she was young and now she's gone. There is a steadily growing group of people I have known who were young and now they're gone; it's a little alarming to think about. All of them had dreams and hopes and ideas and likes and dislikes and problems and fears just like you and I do right at this moment. I seem to think about Alison more now as time begins to close the gap between us and our fates. One of the interesting quirks of the aging process is that events that seemed to have little or no impact at the time resonate with a thunderous importance later on, like an expertly constructed detective novel. I thought it was the relationship with Gillian that was important, but at this point in my life, the half-hour conversation with Alison seems much more significant.

Diana Spencer and I were so close in age that it didn't make any difference, though we had plenty of other differences to make up for it. She was born into the top end of the British class system; I was born into the bottom. She was for the throne, I for the factory floor. She grew up in parties and palaces and titles and sunshine, and I was raised in the grim, damp obscurity of a prefabricated postwar social experiment. She enjoyed the music of George Michael. I did not. I always thought we had absolutely nothing in common, but I wonder about that now. We were rubes, both of us. Products of the class system, even on opposite ends of the spectrum. The Big Fucking Swindle.

I first became aware of her along with the rest of the world when it was announced that she was to be the teen bride to Prince Charles, the heir to the British throne. I didn't pay much attention to royal gossip then, nor do I now, for that matter, but the story was huge because this was the *future queen*. Her face would one day be on our money. It seems odd to think now that if she and the marriage had survived, she'd still be in a holding pattern like her increasingly geriatric ex-husband.

I remember thinking she was attractive. She *was* attractive. She was stunning. The press could not get enough of her. The picture that made all the papers at that time was the one of her wearing a light-colored skirt with the sun behind her showing her legs. An

iconic vision of emerging womanhood. The English Venus, a
Marks & Spencer Aphrodite—wank fodder for the aristocrats and
Cockney cabdrivers alike. There was a suggestion, a giddy insinuation in the tabloids, that with the introduction of this stunning
specimen into the gene pool, at long last we would once more have
a royal we wanted to see naked.

> Years later the tabloid dream would become a reality when
> her younger son, Harry, got a bit toasted in Vegas and let
> his hair down and his trousers off. Personally I think he
> was entitled to do this, and it made me like him. This young
> man saw combat in Afghanistan when he could easily have
> used his privilege to get medals without going near the fray.
> I have had conversations with his brother officers who have
> nothing but admiration and respect for him, and if a front-
> line ginger motherfucker can't get nekkid on leave in Vegas
> and blow off a little steam now and again, then what the
> hell was he fighting for? The security detail were the only
> people I was disappointed in. They should have confiscated
> all the cell phones.

I watched Diana's wedding on a crappy TV in a shitty flat in a
crumbling Glasgow tenement on a damp Wednesday afternoon
in July 1981. I had spent the previous evening at the Hellfire Club
studio, a small, dark, basic but super-cool recording facility in the
basement of a derelict building where a girl I liked was rehearsing
with her band.

After rehearsal we went to the pub and then for a curry before
ending up at David and Jacqui's flat. David and Jacqui were the

owner operators of the Hellfire Club, an interesting artistic couple who were sophisticated beyond anyone I had ever met. They liked David Lynch movies (I had recently seen *Eraserhead* and was still a little rattled) and Brian Eno's ambient albums. They had been to Berlin and Barcelona and Paris and they wore sunglasses in the rain. I loved them and wanted very badly for them to like me, which they seemed to, at least enough to let me sleep on the couch in their living room when it got too late for me to get the night bus back to Cumbernauld. I woke up the next morning and immediately felt relief because by some miracle I had not peed myself even though I'd been pretty drunk the night before. It was going to be a good day. Any time I woke up dry was a good day.

The whole nation had been anticipating the nuptials of Charles and Di for months. Even cynical punks in the West End of Glasgow had become interested enough to turn on the TV and have a look. Tricia, the girl guitarist I liked, turned up and sat next to me on the sofa to watch the show. Again I thanked the gods of continence.

David and Jacqui offered me a croissant for breakfast, but although I was ravenous I didn't know what a croissant was and assumed it to be some sort of a drug, so I declined. It was only when they sat down to eat that I realized my mistake.

"You know, these smell so good. I've changed my mind. I will have a cross ant if you don't mind," I said.

As Diana walked down the aisle of St. Paul's Cathedral, I snuggled on the delightfully dry couch with my cool friends and a guitarist from an all-girl band and ate a delicious pastry which I'd never heard of before. We were just hungover enough to feel cozy as we watched the TV and gleefully mocked the pomposity of the ceremony and Diana for her privilege. As I look back, between the two of us, I had the better of that day. She was nineteen, only a year older than me, but she didn't seem young at all. She belonged to her old husband and her old church and the old families and all the old clergymen who stood around drooling over the rites, half chub under their cassocks at the promise of her fertility.

As the weird, boring Anglican ceremony droned on we were momentarily distracted by an ambulance team that had arrived on the street outside. We watched from the window as they carried out a covered gurney from the facing building. It happened that an old lady had died alone in her house, her demise only becoming evident because her daughter who lived on the other side of the world in California had been unable to reach her on the phone and eventually contacted the police.

I remember how we all remarked on how sad it all was, how poignant it seemed that a forgotten, poor old working-class lady had died like this on the day of the royal wedding. Somebody said they were going to write a song about it, but I don't think anyone did. After the body had been taken away we went back to watching television.

It was eleven years later and Diana and I had both gone through a great deal by the time I met her. Rumors were already swirling about the state of her marriage and she was about to embark on her harrowing separation and divorce. It seemed she had been on something of a roller-coaster ride since the day of her wedding. The joy of the arrival of her sons tempered by the despair of being trapped in a prison of a loveless relationship with their father and royal convention and media attention. I had been on something of a ride myself. Less public perhaps, but bloody awful nonetheless.

Drugs and booze had helped fuel some hilarious and thrilling adventures but ultimately settled in to kicking the shit out of me and ruining my life.

In the summer of 1992 I had been through rehab and was beginning to slowly try to construct a post–alcoholic apocalypse life for myself. I was still very raw and nervous, so when one of the many relentlessly cheery, sober, posh Chelsea girls I had met since drying out asked me to host a charity event benefiting homeless addicts at the swanky Mayfair Hotel in London, I declined on the grounds that I wasn't ready to go back to performing yet. I'd fuck it up in front of all those rich toffs. My friend John, who had gotten sober a bit before me, told me rather emphatically that I should do the gig. He helpfully pointed out it was a charity event, so it was a good cause, and if I did fuck it up then at least I wouldn't be taking any money for it. He also pointed out that people had been kind enough to help me when I was in trouble and this was a good way to start repaying that debt. Basically he shamed me into it. I called back Chelsea Girl and told her I'd do it.

"Fabulous!" she squeaked. "HRH will love you."

"Who's HRH?" I asked.

"Princess Diana. She's the patron of the charity. She'll be there front and center. Actually there's a small reception before luncheon, so you'll be presented. Best behavior, please!" she said, and hung up with a laugh.

I was much more anxious to find out it was a lunch than to find out I'd be in the presence of Diana. Speaking at lunches is far more difficult than speaking in the evening, when the crowd is more likely to be liquored up and relaxed and responsive.

I cobbled together some cleanish material and a cleanish suit and showed up fifteen minutes early to the hotel. There were a bunch of people on the bill. Some speakers talking about the charity's work, some people who had been helped who would give a few testimonials, and a couple of singers for entertainment. It was my job to act as MC—a shaky version of what I'd eventually do on late-night television. A little stand-up at the beginning and string the show together and keep things moving.

My mouth was dry, my palms were sweaty, and my heart was pounding as I stood in the small function suite of the hotel making small talk with the others who would be on stage that day. Not because I was nervous about the imminent arrival of Diana, who would come and talk to us before the show, but because I'd be in front of an audience sober, something I had never done in my life before. This was a very big deal for me. What if I couldn't speak at all? It would be over. I'd have to find a real job doing actual work. Maybe I wasn't really who I always thought I was.

Diana entered the room without fanfare and the whole situation was very informal, there was no bowing or curtsying that I noticed. She chatted to a few different people, mingled really, before I was introduced to her. I don't remember what she was wearing, something bright and luminescent, I think. Perhaps it was she who was bright and luminescent, or maybe that's a trick of my memory which has been assaulted by the imagery of her legend and canonization.

I liked her—as you might expect a young, straight man to like her—and though I'll never know if this is true, I'd make an even-money bet that she liked me right back. I have no evidence to base that on; certainly there was no inappropriate talk or behavior, and maybe her charm and social skill simply made me feel that I was important. But I don't think so.

I remember her eyes and her hair and her whiter-than-white teeth—like an American's—but what I remember most vividly is how easy it was to make her laugh. Everything I said about being nervous or being Scottish or (jokingly) being interested in becoming royal seemed to delight her. I forgot about my nerves while I talked to her; she made me forget myself for a while. I can't say anything much nicer about a person.

The show itself was actually great. As promised, Diana sat front and center and I did the tired salty shtick of comedian hitting on the cute girl in the front row, although I added a mock-respectful Lady Chatterley forelock tug to it all and the crowd ate it up. So did she, dabbing at her eyes with a hankie provided by someone whose job it was to give her a hankie when she needed one. It's a very happy thing for me to make anyone laugh, especially someone who's sad, which I now know she was. I never met her again and am familiar with her story only in the same way everyone else is, but I made her chuckle and blush once and I'm glad I did.

My shaky beginning as a sober stand-up had steadied sufficiently by 1995, allowing me to follow a dream to Hollywood. I left everyone I knew in the UK and headed out to the great American West to make my fortune like some old-timey, baggy-pants immigrant.

The thrill of arriving in LA was quickly tempered by the fact I had no friends there, no family, no one. I was pretty lonely for a bit, and loneliness can lead to strange old thinking which eventually can lead to some strange old drinking, so I made sure I got amongst my own kind at some twelve-step meetings. There were meetings everywhere, all over the town, and it was a process of trial and error to find where I fit best and felt most comfortable. Initially, because of where my apartment was, I attended meetings that were composed predominantly of gay men. This was fine by me; I have worked in show business my entire adult life, it's not like I was around something I was unfamiliar or uncomfortable with.

This was a time when there was still no real or effective treatment for AIDS. At a meeting of one twelve-step group I attended, a young man struggled to the lectern to take his turn to speak. He was clearly very ill and his friends had to help him with his oxygen tank. A little clear plastic tube was attached to his nostrils.

He spoke slowly and carefully, a little about his past and his drinking and drug use. As he spoke, he seemed to rally a little and his sense of humor began to show itself. He thanked his friends for helping him around in his life, showing up for him when he needed them. They had visited him when he has in hospital—"being poked and prodded, and not in a very nice way." They had taken him out to see shows or stayed home and watched movies with him when he was too sick to move. They had shopped for him and cleaned his apartment and even bedazzled his oxygen tank, although he said he had forbidden them from putting feathers on the mask itself, which felt a little too camp—"like I'd been blowing a flamingo."

As he talked, I forgot—it seemed the whole room forgot—that he was desperately ill. With intelligence and wit, he removed himself from the patronizing position of victim. It was almost a shock when he turned to the subject of his imminent death.

He was sad but not bitter, and reminded me so much of the doomed girl I'd met at the party long before. Just like then, I felt embarrassed and uncomfortable. Like I should be ashamed of my health instead of thankful for it. As usual, at least in my head, I had made the situation about me, but I had learned by then that how I think and how I behave don't have to match, so I forced myself to concentrate on what he was saying with that shocking vivid clarity that death brings to the room.

I'm paraphrasing, but this is how I remember it.

". . . When I hear you all talk about your problems with your careers or your relationships I feel so jealous. I don't want to feel jealous; I don't like that about myself but I can't help it. I'm jealous. I wish I had problems; I don't have any problems, I have no problems at all. I'm on a sweet timed morphine drip and I feel nothing but fine, but I am jealous of your problems because your problems are your life. So please, if you can, remember to be grateful for them."

Then he added, "My only regret is that I'm not British because I'd have gotten a hug from Princess Di. Two queens together!"

He got a big laugh from the room. I laughed too. He kept talking and for a while it seemed like the energy of the crowd was feeding him, making him feel stronger, but eventually he had to sit down and be quiet. Pretty soon the meeting ended and I got back in my crappy used car to go back to my small rented apartment to be on my own until the next audition or meeting.

I thought about Diana that night, about what the speaker had said about getting a hug from her. I remembered that when I met Alison, I had been nervous about touching her hand and she had picked up on it. I was wrong about her illness being infectious, just as I was wrong about Diana. She had reached out and touched and hugged and caressed AIDS patients at a time when all the world recoiled from them because no one was sure how the disease was spread. She had brought succor to those in pain and helped remove the stigma of a prejudice. She really did make a difference in the lives of some people who were suffering and who were afraid. That's a hell of a thing.

I thought about my own prejudice about Diana back when I watched her wedding. Because we were from different backgrounds I thought she was somehow less valid, less authentic than me. I bought the lie of class from the other side. For the first time in a long time I thought about the anonymous old lady who had died alone in a Glasgow tenement. What was her name? Margaret, probably. Who'll write her story? I will. I'll make it up and then it'll be true, like a lot of stories.

I very much doubt there is an afterlife, where people move around in slow motion and in soft focus to an Enya soundtrack, but I like to think that somewhere, even if it's just in my imagining or the pages of this book, that all four of these queens are happy and at peace. That they are free from sickness and unhappiness and prejudice and that somehow laughter is possible.

12

Four Kings

"When a man is tired of London he is tired of life." That quote is attributed to Samuel Johnson, who also proclaimed, "The best thing that ever came out of Scotland was the road to England." It is rumored that Johnson had Tourette's syndrome, so there's also a fair chance he also said, "You look like a cunt in that hat," but that's not the point. Clearly he was an impressive but deluded individual given to extreme and controversial proclamations. Luckily his life was chronicled by James Boswell—a Scotsman—who would clean up most of his uttered ravings and make him look even smarter. Perhaps my assessment of Johnson is inaccurate and unkind, the result of a parochial bitterness. I'm prepared to admit that. I have always had a bit of a love/hate relationship with the English, and London in particular. I have always rather loved them and they have always rather hated me.

I have a similar thing going with onions.

London has always had a bizarre hold over me. I think this at least partially because I first became aware of the city and its promise through the firstborn son of the heretic pharaoh Akhenaten, the ancient Egyptian king who bankrupted and almost destroyed his country with the lunatic notion that there was only one god—he is credited as being the first person to have come up with this bollocks of monotheism. Akhenaten got rid of all the old dog-headed, sideways-walking, fun gods and spent nearly all the money in the world building a new religious capital city where everyone had to worship Aten, the sun god, who was mysterious and boring and didn't even have a cat head or wings. As you can imagine, this pissed off a lot of people, so after the old fool died, the clergy reassembled the previous system. In order to appease the high priests and avoid being murdered, Akhenaten's son and heir, Tutankhaten (*"In the image of Aten"*), changed his name to Tutankhamun (*"In the image of Amun-Ra"*—the old god).

> *The British royal family pulled a similar switcheroo in 1917 during the war with Germany when they changed the family name from Saxe-Coburg und Gotha to Windsor so that British people would forget they were German. It worked.*

Tut's shrewd political move was intended to guarantee a long life, but he might as well not have bothered. He was killed either in a hunting accident or by malaria when he was eighteen.

There has been some suggestion that Tutankhamun was perhaps murdered by some of the aforementioned high priests who were still pretty ticked off about his dad's behavior. This notion has been dismissed by serious academics, but then again most ideas are dismissed by serious academics unless they are the ones who came up with them.

The boy king was buried with pomp and ceremony and gold and jewels befiting his rank, and then he and his cache of treasure disappeared into the sands of the desert until Howard Carter, an Egyptologist from London, came poking around in 1922, 3,245 years later. From March until December 1972 the spoils of this most famous of graves were being shown at the British Museum in London in an enormously popular exhibition imaginatively titled *Treasures of Tutankhamun*!

It is almost impossible to imagine an archaeological presentation receiving so much interest today, but this show was huge. In 1972 Tut was bigger than the Beatles *and* Jesus. In the children's comics and magazines that I read (*Look and Learn* and *Sparky*), there were photographs and stories and articles all about the heartthrob teenybopper pharaoh. With his dramatic black eye makeup and his fame and his smooth golden face and his cool aloofness, he was just what I aspired to be. I desperately wanted to go to London to see the show, but I was ten years old and no one would take me. I was crushed. Things only got worse after my mother announced she was going as part of the teacher training course she was enrolled in. I tried all the tricks of crying and huffs and tantrums and passive aggression, but nothing worked. When my mother returned after the three-day trip to the museum in London I was very standoffish with her until she produced the souvenir program she had bought for me at the show.

It was spectacular, a sumptuous, glossy affair full of beautiful photographs and interesting, weird facts about these alien people who had lived so long ago. My mother also brought back a surfeit of tourist crap—tea towels from the Houses of Parliament, a Big Ben snow globe, a tin of biscuits with a picture of the queen on the lid, and a miniature plastic beefeater in a Perspex cylinder. Somehow in my mind this fused the legend and mystery of ancient Egypt with London to form this enchanted, glamorous city that contained all the treasure in the world.

I had heard adults say that the London streets were paved with gold, but of course they are not. They are paved with dogshit, cigarette butts, and used condoms like every other big dirty city, but London in the early 1970s still had the reek of Carnaby Street and the Beatles. Unfortunately, by the summer of 1979, when I finally made my first trip there, I was seventeen and it was a very different place. Punk and Sid were already dead and gone. Margaret Thatcher had come to power and her cold, cruel hand of austerity lay across the land.

> *I think that the rise of the current Scottish independence movement was instigated by Margaret Thatcher and her policies, which were particularly hard on the Scots. Modern separatists are much more inclined to be motivated by economics than by any revisionist fairy tales like* Outlander *or* Braveheart *or by romantic myths surrounding dubious historical chancers like Bonnie Prince Charlie. Like many Glaswegians I have no time for that tosh, particularly Bonnie Prince Charlie, who drank tea as he watched his men die at Culloden, then ran away dressed as a lady to avoid capture.*

I visited London for the first time with Gillian, my first serious girlfriend, and we stayed in separate bedrooms at my uncle Davie's house in Romford, an unremarkable suburb northeast of the city. We took the magical underground railway train to see all the tourist destinations, and even though it was not the wonderland of my childhood imaginings, the bustle and energy of the city were as intoxicating and thrilling to me as New York had been when I went there with my father. It's possible that I would have stayed in London instead of coming to America at all but for a sort of obscure racism, an ugly caste system that is almost undetectable unless you are at the bottom of it.

By the time I was eighteen I was a drummer, and I began to visit London regularly with bands that I was in. We'd make the round trip from Glasgow in rented transit vans full of amps and guitars and drums and luggage and shitty snacks and beer and hashish. It was about as uncomfortable a journey as possible, but I always loved it. The laughs and camaraderie of the road were infinitely preferable to the crappy gigs and apathetic, sparse crowds that we'd play to when we got there. It didn't matter how popular a band was in Scotland, that meant nothing to cool, surly Londoners, but we had to play gigs there since it was the only way to get seen by record company people. Thanks to the Internet and cheap technology, the music business is much more decentralized and democratic now, but back then getting a recording contract was the only real hope you had of recording your music.

My first stand-up comedy performance, if you can call it that, was during Scottish Week at the ICA galleries in London sometime around 1980. It was a half-assed festival of unknown punk bands from Glasgow and Edinburgh that had been invited to play for nothing to arty Londoners who I think viewed us more as curious novelty acts than musicians. In my case they were probably right. At that time, I was drumming with two or three of the groups appearing and was also known as a bit of a party animal. My friends thought that my hilarious drunken antics would translate into entertaining banter for the audience as the roadies switched out the gear between bands. This was my first lesson in stand-up—it is nowhere as easy as it looks. Stand-up should look effortless and cool and spontaneous and easy, but I was sweaty and desperate and loud and, perhaps most importantly, not funny at all. It was the punk rock equivalent of an office worker believing that Bob from accounts is a better comedian than Dave Chappelle because he wore a lampshade on his head at the Christmas party. I was justly shamed and booed by the crowd, and to this day my toes curl a little at the thought of it.

A few years later when I was filling decent-size venues as a stand-up in Scotland and the north of England, I couldn't even get stage time at shitty comedy clubs in the capital city. It was a salutary lesson in the vagaries of show business and also an introduction to how the "old boy" system works in Britain—or at least how it used to; I'm sure everything is egalitarian and fair now, thanks to Twitter and the inspirational messages on Starbucks cups.

I always had a vague, queasy paranoia that all the television producers and bookers and development executives in London were in a loose conspiracy against me, but I realize now how ridiculous that was. They were not trying to hold me back or keep me down. They didn't think about me at all. They couldn't have cared less about me. What I was sensing was the fact that most of them had known each other at fancy schools and colleges in the south; the more successful ones usually were alumni of Oxford or Cambridge. The sons and daughters of the middle and upper classes were more welcome in the field of entertainment than snotty oiks like me. If my sort were to be involved in culture at all it was as pop star or footballer. This was particularly true of the BBC, which, given that it was publicly funded, I thought should have been a little more like any other government-run institution, where you just fill out your form in triplicate, wait three months, and then await delivery of your own TV series.

When I was twenty-four I moved to London from Glasgow in the hope of a "fresh start," or what is more commonly known as a "geographical" in the parlance of those who work with addiction. That is to say, I thought that by moving myself physically to a new location, I could somehow move away from my drinking. But of course, "Wherever you go, there you are," and they have pubs in London too. My drinking didn't skip a beat. Actually it kicked up a notch due to the plentiful supply of cocaine, which is still easily available and wildly popular in the city. As any hopeless inebriate will tell you, cocaine is a spectacular supplement to the old unremitting dipsomania. It stops you from blacking out, which is wonderful. You still behave like a dick but you remember everything. This is very handy in letting you know who and where you ought to avoid for the next few months.

Still, it was in London that I finally quit drinking and spent my first few years of sobriety. I remember how shocked I was that everyone was so much nicer to me and how much easier it was not only to get a gig but to do the job once I had it. This period, between 1992 and 1995, was the most joyful time I ever spent in the city. I had a tiny rented attic flat in St. John's Wood near Regent's Park. In the early mornings I used to listen to the sound of cavalry officers taking their military horses for their daily run. It was the first time since early childhood that I remember being happy.

Professionally, though, I was very impatient and wanted things to happen faster, so obviously LA was a better fit. No one in Hollywood cared if I had been a drunk or came from the wrong social background. In Hollywood the only barometer of success is the amount of money you can make for the studio or network or agent or manager you are in business with. No one gives a rat's ass about your history as long as it doesn't affect the bottom line.

> *This has always been true of Hollywood since the very be-ginning, when the pioneers of the motion picture industry moved to California in order to avoid lawsuits from Thomas Edison, who wanted to charge people for using his patented film camera. Hollywood is a town founded and largely run by disreputable carnies. That is why I think many people in the rest of the United States get so exasperated by moral and political preaching from actors and other entertain-ment industry types. These are people who in earlier times would have been traveling from town to town selling snake oil and stealing pies from your windowsill. The hypocrisy of modern Hollywood sexual puritanism is as ridiculous as the plotline of a Jean-Claude Van Damme action thriller in the eighties. To put it another way, I once had an actress of a certain age who had been a bit pompous and haughty and pleased with herself on my late-night show. I told this to a very famous movie director who had worked with her, and he replied, "God help us when the whores become ladies." That's Hollywood. Nowt as grand as an old tart.*

Although I have lived in Los Angeles since the early nineties I have returned to London many times since, and every time I go, there's always some snub from a maître d' or some awkward mo-ment at the reception desk of some smug private members-only club where successful English people insist on having business lunches to remind me of why I left. For me, trying to get a job in London was like trying to con my way into the first-class lounge at an airport when I only had an economy ticket. Occasionally I could do it, but really only because whoever was guarding the entrance took pity on me or fancied me a bit. Maybe this is true of everything in my life, but I am particularly aware of it in London. "You're just another chippy Scot," Bob Geldof told me when I talked about this with him on television a few years ago. Maybe he's right.

Recently I was approached by a very successful English producer to develop a reworking of an old seventies TV show that I had loved. I was intrigued by the idea and we arranged to meet when he was in LA working on another project. He is a very clever, impressive gent and we got on famously. In the course of our lengthy and wide-ranging conversation he mentioned he had recently been knighted. He was now a "Sir." I congratulated him and told him how envious I was.

"I wish I'd stayed in London. Maybe I'd have gotten a knighthood and been a beloved TV detective by now," I said. I was joking.

"There's still time," he replied. I think he was joking too, but even if not, that could never happen. I have stated many times over in many different places how important the Scottish comedian Billy Connolly is and was to me. To all working-class Scots in entertainment he was like a combination of Jackie Robinson and Elvis and the Beatles. Before Billy there was nothing. I hold him in great reverence not only as a creative genius of stand-up but as an artist who carved his own way through the world. He is also a nice man and a generous soul. Clearly I am not the only person who feels this way about him as he is now not just Billy Connolly, he has been knighted. He is now Sir William Connolly.

When I read the report that he had been given this honor, I was happy for him. But when the photograph of the ceremony appeared online it made me feel sad. Billy, now an elderly and distinguished gentleman, had to kneel on a little blue cushion while Prince William, Diana's oldest boy and heir to the crown, tapped his shoulders with the magical sword, dubbing him a knight of the realm.

I am not condemning Billy for accepting the honor, nor do I think less of him for it, but there is no way in hell that I could or would do it. Not that anyone has ever asked, but I would never take a knee before royalty. Nothing personal; I don't know Prince William, but he represents an outdated, cruel, pre-enlightenment government system that still wields far more influence and enjoys far more privilege than is appropriate. I reject the idea that inheritance is worthy of social status. I resent that the old-boy network propels others forward while leaving others behind regardless of ability. Royalty is the vivid illustration of a system that says you have succeeded because the king notices you.

With the utmost respect—whether you are Ahkenaten, Tutankhamun, Bonnie Prince Charlie, or William Windsor—fuck you, your majesty. The only place I will ever bow to another human being is in a sushi restaurant.

13

Love and Bullshit

The fact that there are many different flavors of love is not news to you, I suppose. I certainly wouldn't dream of trying to define it for you, but my own experience of love has been confusing to me and I suspect I am not alone in this.

First of all, as far as I can tell, love is not all good. Not at all.

I know what it's like to be loved by someone whose love I return, and that is certainly a most joyous state of affairs. Less fun is to be loved by an individual who is disturbed or angry or even a complete stranger to you. I have experienced that too.

I have loved someone who doesn't love me and that is just awful. I have also experienced myriad emotions that I have called love but were actually nothing of the sort. And so in examining my own history with love I think that I have to first look at a problem I have.

I have always had trouble identifying my actual feelings. Sometimes what I genuinely believe to be a certain emotion turns out to be something much simpler or wildly different. For example, when I'm hungry, often the first symptom I experience is not the desire for food but the desire for revenge. I'll think, "I need to set that bastard straight once and for all," when what I really need is a bagel. If I still feel like setting the bastard straight after eating

the bagel, then I will attempt to put my opinion across in a respectful and appropriate manner without spitting poppy seeds and
cream cheese.

Of course, there's always the risk that you'll get caught in the
relief the bagel brings and mistake your rage for hunger, devouring bagel after bagel to feel better instead of confronting that ding-
bat, asshole, childhood trauma, or mime who pissed you off in the
first place. That's how you end up stuck in bed wearing curtains
and cleaning yourself with a sponge on a stick.

It's a balancing act.

My own mother used to say, "Chew down the bad feelings,"
when I was an angst-ridden teen, and she would feed me custard
creams or potato scones. I have no doubt that she loved me and
the rest of her family, but that is terrible advice for approaching a
resolution to an emotional problem. It's not even that effective as
a short-term balm, it's just using biscuits and spuds as inefficient
narcotics.

To my mother, then, my first experience with love.

I loved my mother as much as any child does, but I'm not a
child anymore so it would be infantile and stunted to remain
blind to her imperfections. As I got older she failed to meet that
impossible standard I placed on her, but for a long time I felt
that any criticism was disloyal or somehow *unloving*. I got past that
with a little life experience and a little therapy. Unfortunately I
think my mother felt the same way but was not interested in or
capable of changing her mind about it. She thought that if I was
critical of her or my childhood, it implied that my love for her was
diminished in some way. So, because I loved her, I didn't bring it

up. We didn't talk about a lot of our history, and it created a gulf between us that I don't think we ever bridged, which is sad. I loved my mother and she loved me, but we stopped talking as closely as we could have for fear of that not being true.

My father and I also loved each other, but we never really had intimate conversations so it never became a problem not to have them. Our communications were based on masculine facial expressions, saying "aye" from time to time, and looking at the horizon to make meteorological predictions.

"It's gaunny rain."

"Aye."

Romantic love predictably began to swirl for me with the onset of puberty. I became fixated on girls who I was sexually attracted to and thought the stirrings and aches in my nether regions were the onset of deep, poetic, and hopefully carnal relationships.

Romantic love came and went and there were periods in my life when I genuinely believed my relationship at the time was "it." The "real thing." Real Love. But at this point in my journey, I think that as genuine as the emotion felt at the time, it bears about as much resemblance to real love as the desire for a bagel does to real rage.

My first true Real Love was my first child, which meant the nasty, inconvenient, unpleasant business of genuinely loving another human being without judging them or caring or even wondering if they loved you back. Just Love in all its grisly glory.

I wasn't aware of it at first, there was just the joy of him being born healthy and the seemingly endless sleep-deprived cycle of feeding and caring for an infant. But as he grew, he grew on me in a way I had never before experienced. I began to realize that I had a responsibility toward him that transcended my own comfort.

I believe this is at the core of real love.

By the time my first son was two years old I realized I could no longer live in the same house as his mother, Sascha. You have to understand, I'm a Scottish Protestant; it would have been more comfortable for me to spend my life in a miserable marriage than to break one up. She must have realized this too, because she asked me to leave and I did.

The emotion that I felt for Sascha was not love. I called it love, but I don't think it actually was. I don't believe that I'm saying that just because we have divorced and I have moved on. I don't think it's graceless revisionism—not that I'm not capable of that—it's just that because of the importance to me of the individuals involved, I have had to be much more circumspect about the situation.

The truth is that before we were married I had grave reservations—we were too different, wanted different things, liked different things. She likes a big, busy life full of people, I like a few close friends to visit one at a time a couple of times a year, if that. I found myself getting angry at her for just being who she is, which is terribly unfair, but the truth is she irritated me. Before we got married I told myself this was just "pre-wedding jitters," completely ignoring the fact that I felt them the entire time we were dating and during the ceremony and the entire duration of the marriage. Here's a tip for the kids: don't marry someone if you are annoyed at them all the time. It's a sign.

Now please don't mistake what I am saying here. I am not

saying she's a bad person, or that the failure of our marriage was her fault; I'm saying that I married someone who I didn't want to.

I had done it before, when I was married for a short time when I was twenty-one years old. Why? Why on earth would you put yourself and someone else through that? Why on earth would you do it *twice*? I have asked myself that many times since and all I can come up with is that I felt like I should.

When I was a kid in Scotland I thought marriage would make me more mature, usher me into manhood, maybe slow down the drink and drugs. It would settle me down, as it were. This is of course a terrible reason to get married, and I have since apologized profusely to Anne, who was also ridiculously young at the time.

Yet at thirty-six years old and seven years sober I got married again for almost exactly the same reason. I felt like I should.

Why?

The only answer I can think of is that it wasn't about love at all. It was about the desire for some form of respectability, coupled with the fact that Sascha seemed to really want to get married. At the time, I was too much of a pussy to defend myself against the desires of others and too shut down to recognize my own desires. It was just another angry bagel. I'm glad I married her, because Milo was born and my life changed. I loved someone for the first time, but it wasn't her, it was him.

The inevitable question is that if we—Milo's parents—loved him so much, then why didn't we "make it work"? In truth, I believe we did make it work by not remaining married, by not making him grow up in a contentious environment. By not sending him a message that you have to live with someone you don't love. To those who say "But you made a commitment," I reply, yes, you're right. I made a commitment and then broke it, and it cost me all the money I had and a fair chunk I was yet to make, and it was worth every goddamn penny for both me and my son.

> *I don't subscribe to the notion that saying anything nega-*
> *tive about the other parent is alienating the child, the whole*
> *"you are attacking a part of them." That's horseshit! It's*
> *just another way for narcissists to claim dominion over*
> *their kids. I am not my parents, you are not your parents,*
> *the children of Nazis are not necessarily Nazis, the children*
> *of murderers are not murderers. Likewise, as we have seen*
> *many times, the progeny of great talent is not necessarily*
> *greatly talented.*

And so it came to pass that I was a single dad at forty-two years old, living in a babyproofed bachelor pad in Hollywood. I'd discovered Unconditional Love in the form of my son, but I had given up on Romantic Love with a woman. Then, at last, Megan.

That I loved Megan from the moment I saw her seems a trite and inauthentic thing to say. Certainly I didn't love her then as I do now; that would have been weird and inappropriate and probably would have put her off, but there was something immediately different about her. In my autobiography I described our first meeting in vague terms, but in actuality I remember it with what I believe to be total clarity. I was introduced to her and was a little shocked and intimidated by her beauty. She is remarkably good-looking and this is not an uncommon reaction to meeting her. I tried to be glib and said, "Wow, you are spectacular, we should get married."

I admit it was a douchey, clumsy, arrogant thing to say, but like I said, I was thrown off my game. To my surprise she didn't say no or roll her eyes, but rather commented on my accent and the fact that her family on her father's side was all from Edinburgh. I resisted the Glaswegian impulse to dismiss Edinburgh as a part of England and tried to engage her in conversation like I would a normal human being who was not so clearly genetically gifted.

> *I don't believe discomfort is an abnormal reaction to encountering physical beauty. I think it's pretty typical and often manifests in unkindness. Many physically striking people are extremely insecure about their looks, having been told often that beauty has no real value—it's only skin deep. This is clearly not true or else all models would be broke. Gorgeous individuals are also persistently reminded that beauty has no virtue, which is, I suppose, true, but it's also not shameful. What I'm saying is, if you are young and pretty, lighten the fuck up and enjoy it. And if you are someone who doesn't feel all that attractive, perhaps that's not true, perhaps you're getting the wrong information from those around you. In other words: fuck the haters. The cliché I do believe is true is that beauty is indeed in the eye of the beholder.*

I flirted harmlessly with Megan that night although there was clearly a sexual subtext (I was only hopeful of that at the time, but I know it now). When I suggested that we maybe get out of the noisy party and find a quieter bar or something, she told me no, that she was there with her boyfriend.

"Wait, you're here with your boyfriend?" I asked.

She nodded, looking a little uncomfortable.

"Where is he?"

"He's over there somewhere talking to some people."

I raised my eyebrows in surprise.

"What?" she asked.

"Well," I said, "if you were my girlfriend you wouldn't be on the other side of the room talking to a man like me."

She looked at me in an odd way and I can't be sure, even now, even after we've been together for twelve years, even after she's become the adored stepmother of my first son and the equally adored biological mother of my second, even though we sleep in the same bed every night and share a bathroom, I still can't be sure, but I'd say she made her decision that I'd be her husband right then, when I said that. She says it was earlier in the conversation than that.

I had to wait for her to call me (four months!) and do some fancy dancing and the appropriate amount of wooing, but eventually and finally we got together and have stayed that way. I believe this is it. True Romantic Love.

I absolutely had sworn off marriage. I would have never married anyone except for the person I am now married to, and I would recommend this as the standard for every marriage. Ever.

While getting together with Megan was, for the most part, a sublimely pleasurable experience, it contained a lesson which I suppose I should have learned earlier: not everyone is happy for you to be happy.

Ex-wives, ex-girlfriends, people who are pissed at you anyway, their nastiness is unpleasant but to be expected, I suppose, as part of the rough-and-tumble of life. It was bitterness and cruelty from people who didn't know Megan or me that surprised me.

Megan is younger than I am, twenty years, in fact, about the same age gap between some of the great literary loves. A little more than Mr. Darcy and Lizzie Bennet and a little less than Rhett and Scarlett. It's not an unusual thing historically or culturally. Megan was not a child when we got together; she was twenty-three years old.

Ours is not a coupling without precedence, it contains no scandal, and there was and is nothing illegal or immoral in our relationship, but the reaction from some people was ugly and mean. Bitchy comments from male and female acquaintances about her having a "sugar daddy" (ironically, I was cleaned out from the divorce when I met Megan) or being a "trophy wife," which were insulting to us both.

Megan bore the brunt of it, with comments delivered passive-aggressively and out of my hearing. I am much more likely to bark loudly at you for being a dick than she is. (Don't get me wrong, she'll get revenge on you later, when it suits her. She's scary like that. I respect and fear that kind of patience.) The twisted old shit on the Internet who wanted to "slap the taste out of my mouth" for marrying a younger woman still looms as a vivid reminder of the kindness of strangers.

I don't read the comments anymore.

Until I'd met and married Megan, no one outside my own circle of friends or enemies had ever expressed much of an opinion on whom I had a "right" to love, and I was hurt and angered by this trash. It put me in mind of my gay brothers and sisters who have faced criticism and much worse from opinionated and myopic motherfuckers who are only happy when the world has more hatred and judgment and less love. My own belief is that two adults are allowed to love who they want, and if you don't agree with that, you are a narrow-minded shitfuck and we can't be friends.

14

2008

The big holiday amongst my people is Hogmanay—New Year's Eve. It is a friendly bacchanal in Scotland that has all the advantages of being totally unattached to a religious war from hundreds of years ago, so no matter how drunk everyone gets that evening—and a lot of people get very, very drunk—there is little chance of a fight developing over long-held sectarian hatreds. That's not to say there won't be fights, but they'll be the kind of ordinary drunken fights that nice people have. Like most Scots I have a profound emotional connection to this time of year; it plays into our dramatic, cinematic sense of ourselves and affords us the opportunity to gaze glassy-eyed into the distance and feel emotions about loss and hope that frankly we don't usually have time for. It is a magical time of year and I always want to celebrate it properly. When I was drinking, it was easy to arrange my Hogmanays—just pull a cork and join the party—but after I got sober it got a little trickier. Every year I try to find a way to observe it with joy and solemnity as a proper Scot should. To that end, on Hogmanay 2007 I was ensconced on the flamboyantly picturesque shores of El Matador Beach in Malibu, California.

When I started working in late-night television in January 2005, I had just come through a divorce and was pretty much flat broke. I had made some money on *The Drew Carey Show*, but as anyone who has ever been divorced will tell you, it's not cheap (often they will add, ". . . but it's worth it," which is also true). There's a myth that when people go through the legal untangling of a marriage, they lose half their stuff, but this is a myth that has clearly been propagated by individuals who have never had the pleasure of getting hitched in the great state of California. Half your stuff may indeed go to your former spouse, but the other half will be split up between your lawyer and the legal fees of your partner-turned-litigation-adversary. Your former partner will also receive 40 percent of your annual future earnings for half the time you were married. For example, if you were married for six years, they get 40 percent (gross) of what you earn for the next three after the divorce. The whole process is a terrifying runaway train. At one point, to my immense frustration, I had to pay to have myself investigated by expensive forensic accountants in order to prove to my ex-wife's lawyers that I wasn't hiding money anywhere. In other words I had to prove I wasn't a liar by giving money to people who had called me a liar.

It's not about the money, though. The real battle I had been facing at that time was not financial—I've always had a Pollyanna-ish belief that I'll always find a way to make a living—but rather staving off the rising tide of bitterness that comes with the humiliating task of undoing the Gordian knot of a civil union. I don't have anything against bitterness per se; it has empowered some of my most creative ventures. Resentment is rocket fuel to the artistically inclined—"I'll show those assholes"—but I didn't want the kind of bitterness that divorce was bringing. I had a horrible feeling that if I caved into complaining about alimony payments and child support, I'd turn into one of these shockingly sad

customers with dyed eyebrows and pockets full of Lipitor who
haunt the car washes and coffee shops of LA looking for someone
to read their screenplay or invest in their app.

Megan saved me from that, and I will be eternally grateful to
her for doing so. By the end of 2007, when we had been together
for two years, it seemed clear we were going to get married soon.
We hadn't yet set a date, so for Hogmanay of 2007 I wanted to do
something special for us. In show business terms, I wasn't making
huge sums of money, but it was enough to begin to repair the financial damage that had been done, and even allow the occasional
indulgence. So, three years into my tenure on late night, Megan
and I had enough to rent a little beach house—more of a shack,
really—on El Matador Beach, the least swanky of the Malibu
beaches.

My plan was that, come the chimes of midnight—the *bells* as
they are called in Scotland—we would be sipping some kind of
nonalcoholic fizzy drink on the sand and as the white horses of
the Pacific surf rolled up the moonlit beach we would make romantic proclamations and discuss our future together.

Of course the best-laid plans of mice and men and all that. First
of all, we were not really at liberty to sit on the beach at midnight.
Milo was only six years old and could not be left in the house
alone, even if he was sleeping. Then of course it was very cold, so
who would want to sit on the beach at midnight anyway. Plus we
had our dogs, Maryanne and Gordon, with us. Maryanne is a Jack
Russell terrier, and therefore a hyperactive asshole, and Gordon is
a German shepherd, which means he's nervous and barky and
wants everyone to go to bed as soon as it gets dark. It would be
mayhem with them on the beach at night. And what was the right

time anyway? When would we actually celebrate the New Year? Midnight in Scotland was only 4 p.m. in Malibu. As always when children and dogs are involved, it was too difficult to enact a calm, organized plan, so in the end we settled for walking the dogs at the usual time and letting Milo stay up till 9 p.m. local time to watch the New York feed of the ball drop in Times Square. By 11 p.m. we were all asleep in bed.

I woke up and checked the clock.

It was 12:05. The New Year. 2008.

We had left the door to the balcony open to hear the sound of the surf as we fell asleep. Leaving Megan snoozing in the bed, I got up to walk outside and think my big thoughts as I stared at the ocean. I walked onto the wooden balcony and felt warm, foamy mud envelop my foot. I had stepped into a massive pile of dogshit. Not compact Jack Russell shit, but rather the large, loose, meaty feces of the German shepherd, whose business is more like the product of an overweight hobo who lives on a diet of curried road-kill. It was disgusting. I hate dogshit in the best of conditions— actually I can't imagine what good conditions would be for dogshit, though I don't suppose anyone really likes it. This baby was a spectacular example. Utterly revolting in both texture and aroma. A real prizewinner. A game changer. A Dick Fosbury of a crap. Unable to contain my revulsion, I said—too loudly—"Fuck!" which woke Megan up.

Megan grew up on a farm, so cussing and poop and smells and bottom noises and outdoor sex are no problem to her, thank God. After she stopped laughing, she helped me hop to the shower, where I could scrub the brown death off my toes while she hosed down the balcony.

When we were all cleaned up and back in bed, I started back with the big Hogmanay thoughts. Was this a bad omen? The first thing I had done in the New Year was step in a pile of shit and then say "Fuck." Was the New Year going to be terrible? Megan said I was being silly, that it could just as easily mean it was going to be a great year. She claimed stepping in dogshit is lucky, although that was the first I'd heard of it. She went back to sleep and eventually so did I.

Now, I am not saying that stepping in shit had an effect on the year—I can't endorse the notion that the connection of a human foot and animal dung can alter destiny—but the next twelve months were one of the most spectacular, life-changing periods of my entire life. 2008 was an action-packed fuckruck of a year, at times thrilling and inspirational and at other times heartbreaking and/or terrifying. It was utterly exhausting. Three hundred sixty-five days later 1 felt the same way I'd felt after cage-free scuba diving with sharks in the Bahamas—glad I'd done it but with no desire to do anything like it ever again.

January

My application to become an American citizen had finally been accepted, and in January I was sworn in along with three thousand other new Americans at a fairground in Pomona, California. My fellow immigrants were pretty much all from Mexico, so the affair had a decidedly Latin feel, which I enjoyed very much. By then I'd lived in California for thirteen years, so I was comfortable around Mexican culture and have developed a rudimentary understanding of the Spanish language. The atmosphere was festive and upbeat but also strangely moving with a stirring air of tired and struggling masses yearning to be free, and it was impossible to not think of the waves of immigrant Americans who had come before. It was a fabulous and emotional day, only slightly tarnished by the playing of "Proud to Be an American" by Lee Greenwood whilst giant screens showed footage of Old Glory waving in slow motion.

Now I am as partial to a slow-motion flag as anyone, and had the choice of song been "America the Beautiful" or "The Star-Spangled Banner" or even "Yankee Doodle Dandy" I might have understood, but "Proud to Be an American" belongs to a cheesy, in-your-face genre of cargo-shorts/stars-and-stripes bomber-jacket country music which I'm not particularly fond of. It embarrasses me and makes me feel like I'm in a bad TV movie from the seventies or in a Monty Python sketch mocking American-ness. Voicing this sort of dissent on the day would have been in bad taste, of course, even though it was my right as an American citizen. Instead I sort of hummed along with everyone else who didn't know the words and silently wished we were singing Iggy Pop's "Wild America," which is more the sort of American that I like to think I am.

February

I flew an airplane solo for the first time.

That's right. I flew an airplane ON MY OWN for the first time. After this momentous step I was determined that I would incorporate being a pilot into my life so when I was off playing stand-up gigs in smaller towns, instead of flying into a large airport and taking a regional flight to the venue, I would find a flying school and fly a small plane with a local instructor. Though I had soloed I was still not experienced enough to fly around on my own in a rented plane in an unfamiliar area. This plan would allow me to do my job but at the same time "build my hours"—gain the flight time that all rookie pilots are so thirsty for.

Later in February, I had a show at a casino in Bowler, Wisconsin. Bowler is not a large town; in fact, the showroom of the casino was a large tent with a trailer out back to "relax" in. It was February in Wisconsin, so the word "relax" in this context meant to "experience hypothermia."

I found a small non-towered airstrip nearby and contacted a flight instructor in Minneapolis who was willing to make the trip with me for his usual hourly tuition rate plus "tips." After jetting into the big airport as a customer, I crossed from the main terminal to the general-aviation buildings on the opposite side of the runway to meet an old pilot who for the purposes of this story we shall call Bob. This was before Yelp, so there was nothing really to recommend Bob to me other than I liked the sound of his voice on the phone. He was satisfyingly pilot-y. Big, mustachioed, grumpy Wilford Brimley Republican who smelled like a wet dog. I felt safe getting into the plane with him, and indeed he knew the terrain like the back of his hand. Like most pilots he was a much nicer and happier person once we were airborne.

We flew out to the small strip. I performed the two shows I was contracted to do that evening while Bob shivered and dozed in the trailer "backstage." The audiences at the shows were great and warm and I had forgotten how cold it was outside until we were climbing into the tiny Cessna for the flight back to Minneapolis. I was desperate for a pee before takeoff but there was no bathroom, or even a building nearby, and I didn't want to risk frostbite. Bob agreed. He advised I should hold it for the hour it would take us to get back to the big city.

"Ah wurn't take ma peter out in this—lible to snap off," he advised, sagely, in his reassuring aviator's baritone.

There was no moisture in the air (it was all in my bladder), so with no danger of the plane icing up we punched the throttle and climbed out of the airstrip. Wisconsin in February is fucking cold at sea level but at four and a half thousand feet it is unbelievable. Dante's-deepest-level-of-hell cold. Apocalyptically cold. California-divorce-lawyer cold.

Bob turned on the heater in the Cessna, which anyone familiar with this type of aircraft will tell you is about as much help as opening the window. Cessna planes are excellent; unbelievably durable, reliable, safe machines that all but fly themselves. They are a triumph of American engineering, but for some reason the Cessna company can't make a decent heater. All the heater in a Cessna 172 will do is make you feel like your feet are on fire whilst leaving the rest of you shivering like an anorexic polar nudist.

The flight itself was amazing, a clear moonlit night with a thick blanket of snow on the ground, and it remains one of the most romantic vistas I have ever seen, although it was difficult to enjoy it with my bladder straining to contain its terrible load and my feet reaching reactor-melting temperatures while the rest of me was entering some kind of catatonic shock from the cold. It didn't help that my companion was part man, part damp sofa. Of course, thanks to my stepping in dogshit on Hogmanay, it was at this point that Bob decided to open up to me about his impending divorce.

He talked about how he still loved her but it wasn't going to work out after all these years and that the kids were grown so they'd be okay. He sounded very sad and I can't be sure but I might have heard a sniffle on the headset as he was talking to me. I dared not turn and look at him for fear of seeing an icy tear bounce down his ruddy fat cheek. The way he was talking definitely had an "Oh, what's the fucking point anyway" vibe, which is not what you want to hear from the pilot in command. However, the need to pee was screaming at me more than my own mortality, and after Bob calmly and expertly squeaked the Cessna down on the tarmac, I opened the door and was out and running to the side of a hangar before the plane stopped moving.

It was slightly warmer in Minneapolis but even if it had been colder I wouldn't have cared. I was prepared to risk temperature-induced castration. I unzipped and unleashed the longest pee of my life to this point. It was transcendental. Unbelievable. I was almost ashamed it felt so good. One of the top five physical experiences of my life. It went on and on and on. I can't recall if I ever saw Bob again after that moment. Perhaps he was just a friendly old phantom getting needy travelers to a convenient spot.

March

I had three extremely difficult speaking engagements over the next three months. None of them would pay me any money, but all three were obligations from a sense of duty. (This is how I know I'm sober. Drinking alcoholics rarely, if ever, do anything from duty.)

First I was invited to be the comedian at the Simon Wiesenthal

Center's Holocaust memorial dinner. Of course, being a comedian
at a Holocaust memorial dinner is an impossible task. The whole
affair is somber and distressing, and I should have politely declined, but that wouldn't have been easy. If you live and work in
Hollywood, you are going to interact with the Jewish community,
so I am *mishpocha* by now. My oldest son is Jewish through his
mother, and my brother claims that the Fergusons are the lost
tribe of Israel because we are racked with guilt and enjoy food and
chatting. Obviously to refuse the job would have been wrong. I
thought about trying to wriggle out of it by pretending to be
booked elsewhere, but my agent is Jewish and I didn't think I
could ask her to lie for me to get me out of a Holocaust memorial
dinner. Not kosher, if you'll forgive the phrase in this context.

The committee in charge thought that people could use a little
levity to lighten the mood in an otherwise heavy program of
speakers. I was given the coveted comedic spot right after the
priest who talked about his work uncovering forgotten mass
graves in Poland. I had no idea what to do; there was just no way
to be funny, so I talked about my discomfort and strangely it kind
of worked. The audience wasn't slapping their thighs and hooting
hysterically, but I raised a few chuckles and lightened the mood
long enough for us all to catch our breath.

April

The second of the three speeches. I was the comedian at the White
House Correspondents' Association dinner in Washington, D.C.
Perhaps I should say I was one of the comedians at the White
House Correspondents' Association dinner, as it was the last year

of George W. Bush's presidency and he was always good for a laugh. There was no way I could have refused this job. I had only just become a citizen and it would have been shockingly unappreciative, borderline treasonous.

I have talked and written about that evening at length elsewhere, but it was significant as part of the whirlwind of 2008. The pressure leading up to it contained the combined jackal-like anticipation of both Washington and Hollywood salivating for my failure and disgrace. There was a palpable sense that even my friends were a little aroused at the thought of my massive public embarrassment. It was very stress-inducing. I get hives thinking about it even today.

Before I started speaking that night, I remembered the dogshit on the balcony in Malibu, and it brought me a sense of eerie calm. I can't remember ever being so sanguine before an important gig. Perhaps it was because the event was packed with some of the most powerful and important people on earth at that time, but I felt an odd sense of destiny. Strangely heroic, whether I was a heroic success or a heroic failure. As it turned out, I was neither. I did just fine and didn't get into any trouble or shit my pants, and that would be enough to starve the crones of the chattering set who had been waiting to gnaw the very marrow from my bones.

May

Turned out I did better in D.C. than I thought I did. I had pitched an idea for an autobiography to my agent, the legendary Hollywood uber-yenta Nancy Josephson, who had liked it and said that we were on a roll after the dinner in Washington. She felt that a

book deal would be an easy sell; all publishers were groupies for
politics and we had just scored a goal—or at least, not scored an
own goal—in that arena.

Nancy felt that, given we were already under contract at CBS
Television, we should offer the book to the CBS publishing division first to be polite. We did so and they said they would love to
publish it, and in turn offered an insultingly low sum of money
for the right to do so. Actually I thought it wasn't that bad, but
Nancy said that it was too low and she is very astute about that
sort of thing, so I listened to her. She suggested we go to New York
together and pitch to the big publishing houses there to see if we
could do better. I was already frantically trying to do the late-night
show and play stand-up gigs and remember to see my family from
time to time other than at breakfast, but somehow we found a day
and had a series of meetings with publishers in a small function
room at the Essex House hotel on Central Park South.

I think this was the first time I noticed that fame makes you
funnier. Peter Lassally, the late-night guru and my boss on *The
Late Late Show*, always said that. Fame makes you funnier. He cited
the example of when they used to have Dudley Moore on the Car-
son show because Johnny liked him, but the US audiences were
mystified by his sense of humor and never really responded to
him, but after the movie *Arthur* came out and was a big hit, he
would tell exactly the same anecdotes to rapture and guffaws.

I felt a bit like that at that time.

My previous experience in trying to sell a book (the novel *Between the Bridge and the River*) had been horrendously difficult and
embarrassing, and I had managed to find a publisher only after I
had actually completed the manuscript and been prepared to

accept less money in the deal than I would have gotten for a stand-up on a Tuesday night at the Loony Bin Comedy Club in Wichita.

This was very different. Nancy staggered the meetings every hour and I met with groups of editors and buyers who hung on my every word and grinned and chuckled and all made offers to buy the book. Nancy had a fine old time playing them off against each other in that rarest of events so beloved by agents—a "bidding war."

Eventually we went with HarperCollins, who offered a staggeringly inappropriate sum for what was basically a two-page outline for a book called *American on Purpose*.

Within weeks of the deal being done, there was a massive economic downturn and the executives who had paid too much to me were fired, but it was too late to back out. The company was committed and so was I. Now I had to write a fucking book by the end of the year.

Also in May, the third and by far the most challenging of the three speaking engagements: a best-man speech at a Scottish wedding. My best friend, John, had decided, at the age of sixty, to finally settle down and get hitched to his longtime "bidie-in" (live-in partner), Mary. The wedding was to be in Ayrshire, Scotland, on May 17—my forty-sixth birthday. I hadn't spoken to a Scottish audience, especially an inebriated, boisterous one, since 1994, and I thought they might savage me for losing my accent, which is seen as a capital crime in the motherland.

> *Occasionally the Scottish tabloid press and some numb-skulls on the Internet have taken swipes at me for losing my Scottish accent when I'm talking on American*

television. Apparently that is lost on most Americans, who are convinced that I have a thick Scottish brogue. I have never consciously changed my accent at all, but I accept that I probably sound different when I'm in different situations, given that being understood by the audience is a major part of what I do. I think it would be much more appropriate to attack white British singers who try to sound like black people from the Mississippi Delta in order to sell their records. If everybody has to stick to their accents religiously, then Led Zeppelin should sound like their lead singer is Dick Van Dyke in Mary Poppins. *"There's a lay-dee 'oo knows all that glittahz is ghald an she's climbin' a stahrwhay to 'eaven . . ." (Shout-out to the Proclaimers, who sing like they speak!)*

As it turned out, the wedding was fine and I remembered that telling jokes to an audience of half-drunk Scottish people is like riding a bike. Once you know how to do it you never forget. And it makes your balls sweat.

June

June was pretty quiet. Just the usual five hours of TV a week. And some stand-up shows in Michigan, New Jersey, and Canada.

July

Boston was hot. It's always hot in July. Hot and muggy, although New Englanders always say they don't need air-conditioning because "it's naht nowmally like dis." But it's always like that. Get some fucking AC, Massachusetts, New Hampshire, Vermont, and Maine. (Connecticut has AC because they are pussies, as other New Englanders will tell you.)

I love Boston; Megan has a lot of family there, and my father's mother was a Maguire from Donegal so I fit right in. Actually when my hair is cut short and I don't have a beard, I look like most cops in Boston. When my hair is long and I have a beard I look like an undercover cop in Boston.

For a few years I hosted a Fourth of July celebration from the Hatch Shell outdoor concert area by the Charles River. It's a massive event attended by half a million super-enthusiastic, non-ironic Bostonians. It has the Boston Pops Orchestra belting out old-timey patriotic anthems conducted by Keith Lockhart. It has big-name music acts like John Mellencamp and Rascal Flatts and Neil Diamond, for fuck's sake!

> *The following year, 2009, I actually sang "Sweet Caroline" along with Neil Diamond on stage—he put his hand on my shoulder! "Reachin' out . . . touchin' me . . . touchin' you . . . ," which means, no matter what you may achieve in your life, I'll always be that little bit more awesome than you.*

There are military bands and a flyover by some unbelievably loud fighter planes and an astounding, expensive fireworks display. It's the whole shebang. Fuckin 'Murica! It's televised by CBS, hence my involvement, and to not do it on the year I became a citizen would have been unthinkable. I always had a fantastic time there and I hope they ask me back someday.

On this particular year, because of my very public change in citizenship status, I was also asked to lead the Pledge of Allegiance and make the patriotic address at Faneuil Hall. The pledge was pretty easy; it's a time-tested piece of material and if you just say the words no one is going to be mad at you.

Not entirely true, because some people like to omit the "under God" part. I opted to recite the pledge in its current form. Even though the mention of God had not been added until 1954, I had only recently become American and I felt it would have been a little too soon to start suggesting edits and updates. Also, as long as nobody asks me to define what God is, I have no problem with the word.

Making a speech of your own composition at Faneuil Hall, as many people have no doubt felt through the years, is a bit of a trickier proposition. I'm not a hugely political animal but Boston is, much more so than Washington. Boston is filled with Irish and Italians; it's almost impossible not to piss somebody off as soon as you open your mouth.

Megan and Milo had come along to lend moral support along with some pals who lived locally, General George Casey and his wife, Sheila. George at that time was the head of the Joint Chiefs of Staff of the US Army. Megan and I had become friends with the Caseys when we sat next to them at a table at a USO fund-raiser in Washington. I had been intimidated by the general, who was in full dress uniform that night, until I caught him giggling like a teenage boy when the MC announced the "Silver Beaver" award.

He and Sheila are wonderful, honest, thoughtful people and I wish we had more of them in Washington, or in fact anywhere, really.

If you are a needy vaudevillian looking for validation, the problem with hanging out with General Casey on the Fourth of July in Boston is that the town is crawling with military personnel and veterans and you are never going to impress them as much as a well-respected four-star general, even if he is wearing cargo shorts and a polo shirt. I told George it was like hanging around Disneyland with Mickey Mouse. I have to admit, though, General Casey is an impressive customer; apart from his military career he drinks a pint of Guinness faster than anyone I have ever seen.

I was introduced to the suspicious, civic-minded citizenry by Mayor Thomas Menino, a fabulous and controversial former mayor of Boston who has sadly since passed on. Tommy was friendly and chatty with me beforehand and his introduction was, I realize now, designed to get the audience on my side. I'm paraphrasing but it went along the lines of, "I've met a lot of guys from TV and stuff and a lot of them are jerks, but I just talked to this guy for a little bit and he seems okay."

Then he said my name and I walked to the dais and made my little speech about becoming American and everybody clapped. For a moment I considered running for office, but then I remembered some of the stuff I'd gotten up to in the past and dismissed the notion as unwise.

August

Megan's mother, Linda, lives on a rather idyllic farm in rural Vermont, so we traveled there in order to have a family vacation. My goal on the trip was to get started on writing *American on Purpose*, the book that I was already being paid too much money for.

I had never attempted writing about my life, but I found it strangely therapeutic. Going through my past and looking at my behavior and mistakes was like cleaning the garage. Some things brought back tender or embarrassing memories, but as the process continued I got a sense of clarity and freedom from clutter. As it turns out I would have written the book for nothing. Like I did this one.

September

Writing on the book continued in LA but it slowed down a bit because I was back to the daily grind of the late-night show. The way I did late night was anecdotal and personal; it's a very similar muscle used in writing an autobiography. To add a little extra bullshit in my life I had taken a ten-day run of shows at the MGM Grand in Las Vegas. I'd tape the TV show at five, then take a plane to Vegas, do the show there, stay overnight, travel back in the morning, then tape another TV show and then back to Vegas again and so on. When I look back on this ridiculous schedule now, I wonder what the hell was going on with me. Certainly there was a desperate greed—make hay while the sun shines and all that—but I think there was something else too. Using business and activity to avoid the fear of the real world. Fear of the good and the bad. Megan and I had set a date for our wedding, but my mother was very ill.

My mother had been very ill a few times since she was sixty years old and had always made a full recovery. I remember once a doctor in an ICU said she had half an hour, so I should say good-bye. That had been fifteen years before the madness of 2008. It was generally believed by our family that she would outlive us all, but it was September and the weather was changing, as it always does.

October

I never trusted CBS or David Letterman or TV or show business in general, to be honest. It wasn't that these people or institutions were overtly mean or unkind to me. On the contrary, David had been very supportive of my early tenure on *The Late Late Show*, and CBS had far more important things to worry about than me, so they didn't pay me a lot of notice. Show business has been very tolerant of my failings, both personal and professional. It's just that after the artistic and financial failure of my last movie, *I'll Be There*, I became painfully aware that this whole thing was indeed a business and if you were not helping the company's bottom line you were history. I don't resent this fact, actually I'm quite sympathetic to it, really, having since hired people to do jobs that they either turned out to be incapable of or lost interest in, but I recognize it as an irrefutable truth.

Showbiz people love saying they are a family. "Congratulations from your William Morris family," "Happy holidays from your CBS family," and so on. I suppose it's true, at least in the same sense that the Borgias were also a family.

Anyway, in coming to the conclusion that an executive from a corporation could slit my throat and dump me in the East River at any moment, I had decided that I must attain some kind of autonomy. A defense against the dark arts. There is only one magic that does this for me. Stand-up comedy. Spinning mirth from your shitty childhood and disappointments and frustrations and twisted brain and reaping a sense of creativity and fulfillment and financial independence.

I had stopped doing stand-up for the ten years I was on *The Drew Carey Show* because I was busy with screenplays and making independent movies, but when I started in late night it seemed like a good time to get back to it. Clearly, judging by the show's early reviews, I needed something to help get better at the monologue required by tradition to open every show.

I booked a few gigs at some comedy clubs in 2005 and slowly got back into the game. Soon I progressed further than I ever had before. I felt more confident and comfortable on stage than ever. I moved from playing clubs to playing theaters, and the audiences were getting bigger and more enthusiastic. It helped that the late-night show was starting to make me famous, and fame of course makes you funnier.

By now I was ready to record a stand-up special. A one-hour solo performance that I would shoot in front of a live theater audience. I chose the Wilbur theater in Boston for the filming because I love that venue and I seemed very connected to the city that year. So one weekend I flew out from LA, filmed my first

American stand-up show—"A Wee Bit o' Revolution"—and then
flew back to my day job.

The year was kicking the shit out of me. I was exhausted but
thankfully it was almost . . .

November

I played my first big theater show in New York in November at
what remains my favorite venue in that city, the Town Hall. I've
played Carnegie Hall and Radio City and they are spectacular and
flamboyant, but the Town Hall feels the way I always imagined a
Broadway house would. Also it was my first, and you don't forget
your first (says the man who doesn't remember Doris's name). The
point is, it was yet another high-pressure show that required air
travel and jet lag on top of the very busy day job and the meeting
of the deadline for the fucking autobiography, so by the time I got
to Malibu, where I would spend my first Thanksgiving as a citizen, I was asleep on my feet.

All I wanted to do was rest and hang out with the family.

And I did.

For a day.

We were back at the rented shack on El Matador Beach. We had
liked it and just kept renting for one more month and one more
month. We had finally convinced the German shepherd that shitting on the balcony was a bad idea. We had a lovely, quiet Thanksgiving day by the ocean, but on the Friday after, I got a call from
Janice, my older sister.

My mother's health had taken a rapid downturn.

It was time to come home.

Now.

December

My mother's favorite movie star was Tony Curtis. He had been a guest on the late-night show in November and had graciously signed a framed photograph of himself for her along with a cheeky little note. I had planned to give it to her as a surprise when she came to my wedding, which was scheduled for December 21. I told her about it on the phone as I was on the way to the airport to see her on the day after Thanksgiving and I'm glad I did. I told her I was coming to see her and she said I love you son and I said I love you Ma and those were the last words we ever spoke to each other.

By the time I got to Scotland she was in a coma. When I walked into the room at the assisted living facility, she was lying on her back on the bed, her breathing slow and noisy with the unmistakable rattle of pneumonia. Her hands were clasped across her chest and someone had placed a little wooden cross in them.

My sister Janice was sitting on a chair at the far side of the bed. She was knitting. It's funny, until then I didn't know Janice could knit. My mother used to knit clothes for us when we were kids. I think she liked it; it had a calming, meditative effect on her and it helped with the economic realities at that time. I remember my mother as a young woman, sitting on the threadbare red-and-gray settee in our living room, her knitting needles clicking in her hands as she watched *Top of the Pops* on the BBC with us, laughing and tutting at the outlandish dress and hammy performances of the 1970s pop stars.

I showed Janice the picture of Tony Curtis and she smiled. It felt kind of lame and pointless now, but then again so did everything else. My mum, Netta Ferguson, died within twenty-four hours of my landing back in Glasgow. I don't know if she was aware I made it back in time to see her. Janice says yes but I'm not so sure.

I had to stay in Scotland to help with arrangements, so to keep my mind from turning on me I finished writing the autobiography. I took it all the way to that moment and wrote the last words on the morning of her funeral.

Megan had said we should postpone the wedding, but I refused. My mother would have been horrified by that idea, and I also think I was probably in some kind of shock or denial. I got back to Los Angeles and pre-taped a week of upbeat Christmas shows before heading back to Vermont for the wedding. Looking back on it, I find it sad that no one from CBS or the show suggested I should take some time off. So much for being family, I suppose.

There was a massive blizzard on the day of the wedding. Half of the guests couldn't make it, the reception had to be canceled, and I skidded my truck off the road into a ditch trying to ferry people from a local inn to Linda's house for the ceremony. In fact, if Peggy Benelli, the justice of the peace in Chester, Vermont, hadn't had snow tires, perhaps I would be a single man today, God forbid.

Milo, who was seven years old at the time and had known Megan since he was four, was best man, and Liam, who was yet to be born, says that he watched the whole thing from his star as he waited for us to come and get him. Who's to say otherwise?

The year should have been over. Surely that was enough.

But if the credits don't roll the monster isn't dead yet.

There are certain rites of passage, certain moments in my line of business, when you can think to yourself, *Well, this is it. I made it.* Maybe it's the first time you were on your favorite talk show or you win an award or get blown by a stranger in the bathroom at a movie premiere. Whatever it is, it's ludicrous to think it actually means anything. There is no such thing as "making it" in show business; just ask Steve Guttenberg or MC Hammer or any number of actors who bought a house when their pilot was picked up in May only to have to sell it again when the show was canceled in October. My deep distrust of the game I'm in has led me to accept too many jobs that I knew I shouldn't have because the money was too good to turn down.

Also I'd heard that you know you've made it in show business when you get offered a gig at a casino on New Year's Eve.

So after a Bing Crosby Christmas in Vermont (old, nice-sweater Bing Crosby, not young, angry, beat-the-kids Bing Crosby), I headed off to the Borgata casino in Atlantic City to perform for Hogmanay.

Now, if you have been paying attention you will spot that this is a mistake. There is nothing cinematic and special and Scottish about doing a stand-up show in Atlantic City. I had broken from my own code. The universe showed its wrath at my greed and impudence by sending another thunderous blizzard across the northeast.

I realize that assuming an entire weather system moving across the planet is anything to do with my professional diary is preposterous and I agree, but it sounds nice and dramatic, plus if those idiots who think God helped them win a Golden Globe or find a parking space can claim that kind of bollocks, then why can't I? I particularly don't get the Sports God. If two equally devout players on opposing teams pray for victory, then who gets it? The one who prays better or the one who plays better? It seems to me that when people say they are "giving the glory to God," they are slyly suggesting that not only did they win the game, but they are better friends with God than anybody else and are kind of in the inner circle whilst you are not. The whole thing is so fucking junior high school.

It makes about as much sense as believing that stepping on a dog's crap on New Year's Eve will alter your destiny.

The weather was so bad that flying was impossible, which meant I'd have to drive in order to make the show. I decided it best that Megan and Milo stay behind because the roads might be treacherous, which they absolutely were. Bloody awful. The only vehicle on the farm that was halfway up to the task was the F-350 truck that Linda uses for animal feed. We loaded a ton of logs in the back for ballast and I set off into what became an eleven-hour trip from Chester, Vermont, to Atlantic City. It was a horrendous and stressful drive on roads that were as slippery and deadly as a greased-up Nazi sniper. I arrived at the casino with just enough time to shower and change and give one of the shittiest performances of my sober life. If you were at the show that night I apologize. No refunds, though; I did the best I could!

The New Year chimed as I was on stage and the audience and I gave thanks that we could end this thing with dignity and good-will, wish each other well, and hope for better times ahead.

Hogmanay had come and gone, the whole year had come and gone, with me hardly recognizing its significance and impact. I don't live like that anymore. I don't run frantically from pillar to post anymore. These days, if you booked me and the weather is too shitty, then expect a phone call to cancel.

After a few hours' sleep in one of the casino hotel rooms, I headed back to Vermont. The roads had cleared a bit and the drive was less dramatic, but halfway home I accidentally dropped my cell phone into my coffee cup and it died. Therefore Megan couldn't reach me for hours and became convinced I'd come a cropper on the icy freeways.

By the time I got back, everyone, including me, was frazzled and tired and upset.

That's when I started to think about quitting late-night TV. That's when I started imagining a life without a pathological, ad-dictive attachment to work.

For someone who supposedly had embraced a sober life, my entire mode of existence had become downright *intemperate*.

What I'm saying is I'm not available on Hogmanay. (Unless it's for *a lot* of money. Let's not go crazy here.)

I also make sure the dogs have pooped before I go to sleep.

15

Learning to Fly

I've heard it said that Fear is a shape-shifter, constantly coming at you in different guises to throw you off guard. I think there is an element of truth to that, but it also implies Fear is an enemy with a malevolent purpose, an evil and cunning plan to destroy you. I think that is hogwash. That is just the kind of thing that Fear would have you think. That it is big and scary and powerful and could get you at any minute. Fear would have you believe that it starts with a capital letter, but it doesn't, not unless you put it at the start of the sentence or name your cat after it. Fear is not a proper noun. Fear is just *fear*, just another workday noun or sometimes verb trying to find its place in the lexicon. Like all bullies, it wants you to believe it's tougher than it really is.

I am not for a moment suggesting that fear can be "conquered." I find that whole notion to be ludicrous. Claiming to have conquered your fear is like claiming you have conquered hunger or lust or tiredness. Fear is useful; it's telling you something, but it is a far from reliable messenger.

I fully admit this sounds trite, the kind of thing an unqualified hack would say on daytime TV. But what I mean is that for me, what I think I am afraid of often isn't what I am actually afraid of.

To put it another way, when I'm afraid, I have learned not to accept the first explanation that my brain comes up with. It has cost me a lot of time and distress and money to reach this point, and I have a horrible suspicion that I might have ended up here anyway just by getting older. But let's dismiss that as the pointless negativity of a narcissistic mind in reverse and let me try to explain.

I used to describe myself as someone who was afraid of flying. It's a common enough fear that there are courses and apps and treatments for it. You can even get a doctor to prescribe sedatives for it. It is viewed as a legitimate, understandable, relatable fear. It's explicable in an emotional sense: the very idea of being so far above the ground in a pressurized tube moving at incredible speeds, dependent on machines and pilots that you know very little about, sounds extremely dangerous. Except that it isn't. The earth is hurtling through space at speeds much faster than any airplane could hope to travel and is equally dependent on the laws of physics to maintain its trajectory. It's not any more rational than being afraid of sitting down. Mathematically you are as likely to be struck by a comet as to die in a plane crash in a modern commercial airliner. Six units of alcohol a week are more dangerous than flying, and plenty of people beat that mark.

Fear doesn't deal in fact. It lives in untruth and rumor, like a modern politician. It's a voracious weed that needs just a whiff of uncertainty to thrive, because fear needs to conceal itself from plain sight in order to be really effective. A capricious god whose mind you cannot know, a monstrous foreigner in a far-off land who wants to harm your children. What is hiding in the shadows? Usually nothing.

You can't see how the air keeps the plane up because the air doesn't keep the plane up. Speed keeps the plane up, but the speed is imperceptible because the ground is too far away. And what about terrorists or thunderstorms or turbulence or snakes on the plane?

When I was terrified of air travel, for days or sometimes weeks before a flight I would torture myself with flamboyant imaginings, fiery wrecks, weeping loved ones left behind. I knew that the chances of my dying in a plane crash were infinitesimally small, but that was absolutely no consolation whatsoever. The chances of me going to America and getting a job on a sitcom were infinitesimally small, as were the chances of that sitcom staying on the air for a season, never mind nine years. The chances of getting another job as a late-night host are infinitesimally small. Actually, the chances of the particular sperm that produced yours truly impregnating the uterine wall of my mother were spectacularly small. The odds game is no fucking help at all. If I don't actually get on the plane, the chance of my dying in a plane crash disappears completely. Unless a plane fell on my head, which is about as likely if you live in a big city. Which I do.

> *I'm beginning to scare myself as I write this, imagining that I will die in a plane crash or by being struck by a plane or a comet by the time you read this book. Perhaps this suggests that I don't fear death as much as I do irony.*

I talked about this fear in stand-up and on my late-night television show, mining my fear for laughs and empathy as vulgar entertainers are wont to do. I mocked those who were unafraid, implying that they were dumb or not in possession of all the facts, making my fear look like the more reasonable option. Another trick used by comedians and politicians. Trouble is, sooner or later, if you mock something long enough you are going to rub up against someone who strongly disagrees with you. Someone who loves the object of your scorn. In most cases it results in nothing more than a mean tweet or a heckle, which can be easily dismissed, but every now and then you meet someone or something that requires you to rethink your position. In this particular instance, the motivator of change was an impressive and majestic, rarely occurring natural phenomenon known as a *Kurt Russell.*

Kurt Russell is a full-blown American movie star in the most traditional and proper John Wayne sense. He's a maverick with big muscles, peepy eyes, and great hair. Sometimes he has a mustache, sometimes he doesn't—*you'll never know when it's gonna be there!* He doesn't give a good goddamn about your conventions or manifestoes of political correctness and he's not afraid of shit. In various motion pictures he has shot bad guys, shot good guys, killed aliens, had aliens kill him, saved the day, ruined the day, kissed sexy women, and had them betray him. He's been a soldier and a sportsman and a cop who doesn't play by the rules. He's worn an eye patch in three (THREE!) different movies. He's been Wyatt Earp once and Elvis twice (not in the same film, although that's something I'd like to see); he's acted with animals and children and even Sylvester Stallone. This is a forceful and charismatic individual.

But though Kurt Russell is a movie star for his job, his real calling is being an aviator. He loves to fly and he's good at it. He once told me that the real reason he acts in movies is to pay for fuel.

In 2007, the first time he was a guest on my late-night show, the conversation turned to flying, as I knew it would, to facilitate some

good-natured comedic sparring on the subject (we're both profes-
sionals). But things did not go the way I expected. He didn't mock
my fear or tell me I was wrong. He just told me I had misdiag-
nosed my symptoms.

"You're not afraid of flying," he said in his gravelly Kurt
Russell-y way. "You're just a control freak."

I questioned how he could possibly know that about me given
the recent nature of our acquaintance, and he told me that he had
been on jury duty recently and in order to pass the long, tedious
hours he had spent sequestered he had read a novel I had recently
published—*Between the Bridge and the River*. He declared that it was
clear from my writing that that was what my problem was.

"Also this show has your name in the title. Control freak," he
said again, getting a laugh from me and the studio audience.

I was momentarily struck dumb with vain pride—*Kurt Russell
read my book!*—and then was so taken with the idea of Kurt Russell
on jury duty that the conversation swerved in that direction and
away from aviation. But a seed had been planted, not in my brain
but in Megan's.

We were not yet married, but it was on our horizon and we
both knew it. We'd discussed it, it was agreed. So she knew that
part of what she was signing up for was a life of dealing with a
twitchy nervous wreck sitting next to her on airplanes. She saw
the interview with Kurt and decided that for my upcoming birthday, she'd give me an escape from my fear. She got in touch with
him after the show and between them they conspired to get me
flying lessons. Kurt found an instructor at a local flying school
who he thought would be the right fit for me.

They reckoned if I knew more about it I'd feel better. Megan agreed with Kurt's analysis of me, although I maintain that if you enter a conspiracy to procure flying lessons for someone who is afraid of flying, maybe it's you who's the control freak, or perhaps just a sadist. Either way it works for us.

> *Megan is from an aviation family. Her father flew gliders, which no sane person would ever do, and her grandfather frequently buzzed the farms of New England in his old Boeing-Stearman, shocking onlookers by thundering through the arches under the French King Bridge in Massachusetts. He came by this kind of thing honestly, having been a pilot in B-29s at the tail end of World War II and a flight instructor during the Korean War.*

From the first lesson, I sensed there was something of a change. I wasn't frightened anymore, I was fucking terrified. I hated the takeoff. Hated it. Actually I was close to pooping myself on the taxi to the runway. The plane was tiny and hot and had no AC and it was already ninety-five degrees. I was in a tiny Cessna 172 piloted by a grumpy, beefy, extremely hirsute instructor out of Van Nuys's Encore Flight School at Van Nuys Airport in Los Angeles. My senses were heightened with terror. I remember being very conscious of the pilot's shoulder hair that was visible beneath his nylon shirt. I felt the shirt (and probably a bit of the hair) crinkle against my shoulder in the tiny cockpit. It was all noisy and hot and hairy and crinkly nylon; I imagine a panic attack in Studio 54 in the late seventies would have felt much the same.

My mouth was dry and I was sweating like an overweight drug mule at Turkish customs. My heart was pounding as if I were breathing pure amyl nitrate instead of the earthy musk of a fat man who lived alone.

The air was bumpy and tossed the little plane around as we climbed out of runway 16 R and headed to the coastline. I nervously asked about every movement and every sound, and the old pilot told me that he could turn around and land if we wanted.

"Don't we have to burn some fuel off first?" I squeaked.

"Not that type of airplane. Good question, though," he growled.

For a narcissistic control freak this tiny morsel of taciturn praise was sufficient to allow me a quick steely glare out the window to my side so that I could pretend for a moment that I too was a grizzled cigar-chomping he-man who could keep his head while engines failed and wings fell off. See, pilots are cool. Not on the ground; most of them are geeks who will actually argue—and I'm not kidding—that pocket protectors are a great invention. But when you're flying a plane, no matter who you are, you're cool. It's a scientific fact. And I think that was enough to keep me going back at first. That and the overhead switches (there are no overhead switches in a Cessna 172, but I supposed I'd work my way up to them). The only thing that could possibly be cooler than overhead switches would be Steve McQueen using overhead switches to escape from Nazis. In a flashback sequence.

For some reason that I still can't explain, I kept returning to the airport until, and any pilot reading this will know what I mean, I started looking up. I still do. Whenever I hear any kind of aircraft, and I hear a lot living in LA, I look up. I look up to see the plane or the helicopter, to see if I can identify it, just because I have to see it. Every pilot I have ever met looks up when they hear something in the sky, and when they don't hear anything they look up to see why. Almost as soon as I started confronting my fear, I started to look up, which I think is lovely.

During my flight training I felt that I was learning something important. Not just the technical stuff about airspeeds and the glide ratios and stalls and how to control the aircraft and read the instruments in the cockpit, but also information about the universe which we inhabit. About weather and how it's formed and how it moves across the earth. About the magnetic pull of the poles and gravity and, surprisingly, the utter deadliness of arrogance.

Perhaps it's not too surprising that aviation contains a lesson on the dangers of overconfidence if you consider the ancient Greek myth of Daedalus and Icarus, the father-and-son team who through some long-forgotten technique managed to construct functioning hang gliders from eagle feathers and wax. Daedalus, the father and supposedly older, more experienced aviator of the two, warned his son not to fly too high because he'd get too close to the sun and its temperature would melt the wax and his wings would fall apart. The brash youngster didn't listen and the inevitable happened, plunging him to his grim fate as Charon's next passenger. The story is of course a parable about youth versus experience, and whilst the geezer in me celebrates the idea that by being older I'm somehow smarter, it's probably worth pointing out the scientific inaccuracy of the tale. As you fly higher, the temperature drops, and therefore the wax on the wings would be unaffected. It's much more likely that Daedalus, staying near the heat and capricious nature of the winds nearer the ground, would be the one who would come a cropper. Or as every pilot knows, altitude is your friend. There is much less to hit up there.

Even with the knowledge that Daedalus's science was
wrong, the parable still holds up as a warning against ar-
rogance. Just because you are older doesn't mean you nec-
essarily know better.

What flying taught me wasn't just how to control an airplane. It taught me about perspective. Not just the view from the plane but about myself, where I am in the world and the extent of my abilities. It taught me to be honest about myself.

For my entire life I have said many things about myself without having any idea if they were true. Sometimes they were downright lies.

"I wasn't there."

"I just had two drinks."

"A hobo peed on me."

I have told employers that I could easily ride a horse, swordfight, host a late-night show, whatever the situation required. Those statements would have been much more valid if I'd added, "If someone teaches me." But I always left that part out.

In show business you bullshit to live. In aviation if you bullshit, you die. I might want to tell a fellow pilot or a passenger that I know how to handle a given situation, but if I'm not telling the truth I would probably kill us both.

The name that always comes up is John F. Kennedy Jr.

Mr. Kennedy had everything to live for: love and money and kudos and connections. All the friends. But he made a mistake. Actually, according to the accident investigation, he made more than one, but his fatal mistake was that he overestimated his skill.

He continued VFR (visual flight rules) flight into IMC

(instrument meteorological conditions), which is very, very dangerous. It's Russian roulette. Basically it means that he flew into a weather situation that required him to fly the plane relying only on its instruments. This is easily done by those who have received sufficient training, but Mr. Kennedy had not yet reached that level and unfortunately smashed himself, his young wife, and her sister into the Atlantic.

That tragedy with its Icaran echoes resonated all the way into my flight training. I discussed it with my instructor, who was far less gentle about Mr. Kennedy's decisions that day than I have been here. To illustrate what had happened, he re-created a similar situation during one of my lessons. He told me to close my eyes and fly the plane based on how it feels. He asked me to make a slight right turn whilst keeping my eyes closed. I did so, and after the turn I thought I was flying level, but I had inadvertently tipped the plane into a graveyard spiral, the same situation that killed Mr. Kennedy and his passengers. My instructor quickly and efficiently restored the plane to level flight, but the lesson had gotten through to me. How you feel is not necessarily how it is. In fact, going by feel without having an idea of where you are in the scheme of things will often get you in very big trouble in life as well as in aviation.

I did not know JFK Jr., and I certainly would wish him and his passengers no harm, but I think with a healthy dose of fear, self-honesty, and perspective they would all be moving around today. Fear is not necessarily your enemy. Fear can lead you to the truth about yourself.

I don't seem to have much time for flying these days. The only chance I get is to sit in the big, rattly commercial airliners we all are familiar with, but there is a Boeing-Stearman for sale that I have my eye on. By the time you read this I hope to have quit the daily radio show I do, in part because I want to learn how to fly that plane.

I want to learn and continue to learn. It's the only way to stay alive.

16

Therapy

Contrary to the prevailing wisdom of dance movies, lessons gleaned from greeting cards, and Oprah's messages on Starbucks to-go cups, I do not subscribe to the notion that you can do anything you set your mind to if you *believe* in yourself (whatever the flat fuck that means). I think that if you possess ambition beyond your capabilities, it is not only a recipe for bitterness but an unattractive lack of humility, which can be charming in the young but depressing in those of us who are less rosy cheeked. The American Dream says that you can be a big success no matter where you start out in life and I believe that to be true, but you are not going to be a great singer if you're tone-deaf. Actually that's a bad example, given the advances in recording studio technology. Okay, how about you're never going to be a star in the NBA if you're five feet tall. Success requires adapting to and working within your limits. Pushing your limits is essential, but seeing the world realistically also helps.

I understand the root of this idea that you can be anything you want to be. It's a product of the comparatively new tradition of respecting and encouraging children and trying to make the process of growing up less traumatic. Now this, to my mind, is indicative of a great leap forward in human thought, but as with most good things you can get too much of it and it can make you sick.

Case in point: the disproportionate number of mediocre millennials who believe the sun shines out of their Instagrammed asses— Bah! Get offa my lawn!

I watch my boys be educated in the progressive manner of Californian private schools and I am delighted for them, actually jealous, if I'm honest. This whole "not beating the children with leather belts until they piss themselves with fear and shame" system is very different to my early life experience. But part of me (and I admit, probably a very sick part) fears that all this understanding and positive reinforcement may be turning them into pussies. I keep my mouth shut about this because there is another, healthier part of me that realizes that the sick part is a fucking asshole and shouldn't be allowed to spew his retrograde toxins into the bright pastel classrooms of the modern world.

One of the great temptations of age is to assume that because you lived through a certain event or events and survived, then your children must do the same. It's a well-meaning if erroneous position to take. My children's lives have very few of the dangers that my childhood contained, but they have others that are much more difficult for me to see. That's the whole idea behind listening to them, I suppose.

My parents were locked into the idea of comparing my childhood to theirs. For example, when my parents were children there were Nazi bombers flying over them at night trying to kill them in their beds. Therefore any childhood in which you were not being attacked routinely by the Luftwaffe must be an idyllic one. It's all perspective.

Please understand, I am not whining about my parents being insensitive, and I actually see their position as extremely reasonable. I'm just trying to figure myself out so I pass as little of my crazy as possible on to my kids.

So what I'm saying is, I spend a lot of time in therapy.

I like therapy. I enjoy the experience of discussing my problems with someone I trust to take, if not a totally impartial position, then one which skews in my favor most of the time. I believe therapy to be like marriage or making movies. It's a completely pointless exercise unless you cast the right people. A bad therapist, and I've met a few, is much worse than no therapist at all.

"What's the difference, Craig?" I hear you ask shyly from beneath your tinfoil hat.

Well, I'd say a bad therapist is someone who thinks they know how you should live, someone who thinks that their moral compass is more accurate than yours and who believes they are smarter than you because you are in some sort of distress or discomfort. This kind of douchery is fairly common among therapists I have met, and although some people may enjoy being bossed around by a sanctimonious cunt, that's never really been my thing. I believe that a good therapist is someone who, for want of a more accurate expression, "re-parents" you as an adult. Someone who listens to you describe what you believe is your problem and then offers a different perspective. Perhaps, with a little luck and a lot of skill and patience, that new perspective will help you reach an insight which in turn offers you relief.

Please understand, I am not talking about the treatment of mental illness here; that is a field which I am unqualified to discuss. I'm talking about therapy as a life tool, not in its application as a treatment for depression or other medical conditions. Unlike many people who appear on television frequently, I do not believe that I am a doctor just because I like the sound of my own voice.

I also believe therapy should be private. Like pooping or sex, it's messy and undignified if you're doing it properly, so in order to maintain a shred of human dignity in this overexposed culture it should be confined to a therapist's office. (Therapy, that is, not pooping or sex, although I'm sure that is available somewhere in Los Angeles.)

I do not believe therapy should be done on television, and it certainly should never be attempted without the consent of the patient. In other words, any attempt to analyze someone you have never met from behind your desk in a television studio is totally worthless. Narcissistic media quacks who call themselves doctors based on a shoddy PhD they got at some dodgy college, and who assume they understand the mental condition of a pop star or actor they don't know, are not therapists, they're just assholes. They are just media clowns like myself. Just entertainers. Real therapy is not for show.

I'd actually say that trashy simulated concern in the media helps perpetuate the myth that therapy is somehow self-indulgent. I suppose by nature it is a little, but so are all attempts toward better health, like brushing your teeth twice a day or getting a little exercise now and again.

I have been seeing the same therapist for years now. Her name is Andrea and she is a diminutive and intensely practical Jewish woman from Chicago. She is in her sixties and has grown children and has been through a divorce. There is nothing—believe me, I have tried—nothing I can say that can shock her. It is a mark of her professionalism that I actually know relatively little about her life, whereas she could probably write my memoirs more accurately than me.

Sometimes I go a lot—once a week—and sometimes I don't see her for months. It really depends on work and family schedule and how committed I am to driving across to the Westside of LA, where her office is. Sometimes the psychic distress of the fucking 405 is far more intense than I can drum up from my own dark reservoirs of pain.

Coincidentally, it was on the freeway when I think I first noticed the effects of receiving therapy. I was headed to Warner Bros. one Saturday morning to see the rough cut of a movie I had written and starred in, *The Big Tease*. It's a comedy mockumentary about a camp Scottish hairdresser's adventures in Los Angeles. The movie had not been released yet, so I was in that happy place that all filmmakers experience, between wrapping the shoot and the first reviews when you believe you have a monster hit on your hands (I did not, but although the film was not a financial success I am proud of it and it makes me laugh so fuck you).

I was feeling quite the Hollywood mogul, singing along with Dean Martin as he asked "Ain't that a kick in the head?" from the CD player (it was quite a while ago) when just at the high-speed on-ramp on the 101 near Barham, I saw a white panel van careen across two lanes and slam into the side of a crappy old Toyota.

The cliché is true, everything really did go into slow motion. Dino even stopped singing, and in what I remember as total silence I watched the Toyota become airborne and somersault gently in midair before landing on its roof about fifty feet in front of me.

Luckily I drive like an old lady; I habitually observe braking distances and the "Highway Code" that I was taught in Britain.

As the roof of the Toyota slammed onto the tarmac, the slow-motion camera was switched off and all the sound came back—the screeching protests of my own brakes and the cars behind and to the side of me. All the vehicles stopped, which if you know Los Angeles tells you how serious it was. I looked on in stunned shock as the white van, the cause of the accident, sped away from the scene.

Like everyone else I got out of my car and looked across to the Toyota.

I really did not want to go there; the car was smoking and its wheels were still spinning and it just looked for all the world like cars do in the movies before they explode.

I really, really did not want to go over there, but through the chaos and noise and radiator steam I could see in the back seat of the car there was a child seat. It was occupied. I can still see them now, those two chubby little knees.

I really, really, really did not want to go over to that car, so I was surprised to find myself running as fast as I could toward it shouting, "fuckfuckfuckfuckfuck," and thinking, "not the face not the face not the face!"

I reached the car at the same time as another guy, who seemed about as happy to be there as me. Inside there was the driver, a Mexican man, with a boy who looked about ten in the front seat and a little girl in the child seat in the back. Everybody was conscious, everybody wearing seat belts, everybody looked okay, there was no blood. The little girl wasn't even crying.

It was a two-door car and the passenger-side door was pretty banged up, so I unhooked the driver's seat belt and started to haul him out. He was having a hard time moving. He was almost rigid, gripping the wheel. He kept saying:

"I'm okay, I'm okay."

I wasn't really in the mood to chat about how he was, so I said, more forcefully than I would have in less adrenaline-heavy circumstances:

"Dude, you are upside down in a piece-of-shit car on the 101. You are a long fucking way from okay!"

This seemed to bring him round, and he yelled, "Get my kids, get my kids out first."

I told him he had to get out so that we could get his kids, and he grasped that and scrambled free. We got his boy and his little girl out of there, and there wasn't a scratch on any of them.

Shocked as shit, for sure, but not a scratch.

Everybody got to the chain-link fence at the side of the road, and after a moment just looking at the car, which never did explode, the little girl started to cry and the world seemed to start back on its axis. Almost immediately, with their customary sensitivity, the LA drivers started moving and driving around the scene, keen to get to whatever appointment was so important that particular day.

The guy who ran to the car with me got into his car and drove off, but I stood with the shocked family till the cops arrived. I can't remember giving a statement or even talking to the guy or his kids afterward, but I'm sure I must have done. All I remember after that is that as I drove away I suddenly became aware of a sense of self-hatred. Real loathing. It wasn't quite an actual voice in my head, but it was close. I remember it being a profoundly vivid thought delivered in a nasal and aggressive Glaswegian accent. "I suppose you think you're great. Mr. Fucking Freeway Hero. Hah! You are a phony piece of shit."

Now I believe, had I never received therapy, I would have acted exactly the same as I did that day. I believe that I would have, against my more selfish instincts, run to that car and helped get these people out of there. The only thing therapy changed was my reaction to the "voice" that condemned and mocked me as the phony piece of shit.

I laughed.

In my car, alone, after a scary accident on the freeway, I laughed and then said out loud:

"Nope, you're going to have to do better than that," which may make no sense to you but it made me feel better.

The next thought I had was: "That was scary, you need beer."

And I laughed at that too.

When I got to the screening I had a nice cup of hot, sweet tea.

17

Resentment

Being famous is shit. I believe there was probably a time when it was cool, perhaps during the silent-movie era, when you could parade around your Hollywood estate sniffing nonaddictive cocaine from the heads of bald midgets—that term was still acceptable then—and getting steaming drunk every day before noon (interesting that I should associate "cool" with pathological addictive behavior and casual cruelty toward little people; maybe I should examine that in therapy). But those days are long gone, and being famous now is extremely uncool.

Just look at the people who are famous: idiots, pimps, whores, and killers. Stephen Fry once described fame to me as feeling like the early stages of dementia. Everyone knows your name and what you've been up to but you don't even know who they are.

Fame is certainly an odd commodity, but a commodity it is. If you use it correctly it can be converted into cash and prizes. For example, take tabloid fame, or "famous for being famous." This is to my mind the most loathsome form of fame, yet my guess is that it is the one that the majority of people, particularly those who are currently young, aspire to.

The most glaring—and certainly financially successful—contemporary example of this kind of fame would be Kim Kardashian, who first came to the attention of the masses as a young woman who enjoyed going to parties and clubs with a much more famous young woman who also enjoyed going to parties and clubs, Paris Hilton. Paris Hilton is still famous but she is no longer *current*. Kim Kardashian is *current* as of writing this, but of course there is no guarantee she will be by the time it reaches print.

Current is a subset of famous. It could also be described as "hot" or "interesting to the bovine kashkas who pore over the drivel written in the *celebrity* press." Kim Kardashian's big break into fame came when a sex tape she made with her former boyfriend was "leaked" to the tabloids.

I've seen the tape, and it's a rather tame affair. Even when she gets peed on, it all seems depressingly dumb and joyless, although why I'd expect getting peed on to be clever and cheerful I'm not really sure. The only other leaked sex tape I've ever seen, the one with Pamela Anderson and Tommy Lee, is far more exuberant and fun. It's got pizzazz and humor. It's showbizzy! First of all, it's on a boat in the sunshine, Mr. Lee has a hilariously outsize penis, and then there's Ms. Anderson's colossal breasts, which are garden-fresh from the surgery. It's like an amateur porn cartoon starring the Three Stooges, who have been replaced by Ms. Anderson's breasts (Moe and Larry) and Mr. Lee's penis (Curly). Nyuk! Nyuk! Also, with the Pamela Anderson/Tommy Lee tape, you get the impression that they genuinely like each other and that the tape was not made with any future "leakage" agenda (not that I'm suggesting the

Kardashian one was, for legal reasons if nothing else). Sadly
Mr. Lee and Ms. Anderson are no longer current, to us or
each other.

Ms. Kardashian is extremely current. "Current" is actually more important than fame itself because if you are famous but not current, then you are a shameful failure.

The equation is: Fame – Current = Failure (Shame). I'm sure there are much more current sex tapes and famous-for-being-famous candidates I could use to illustrate this equation, but I'm not a fucking gossip columnist and the equation applies whether we're looking at last year's news or next year's. All of this refers only to tabloid fame, of course. Historical fame is a little different. Isaac Newton is still famous and respected even though he's no longer current, Neil deGrasse Tyson being the hot bitch du jour.

My problem with any fame I've experienced is the inconsistency in which I have achieved it. I've never been famous with the *TMZ* crowd, thank *(insert preferred deity or lack thereof here)*. But even though it's something I've never aspired to, I've occasionally felt embarrassed or ashamed by that, especially when I run into someone who wants me to be more famous than I am.

Devotees of tabloid fame refuse to accept that there is any other kind, and if they don't know who you are, then you don't exist. I was once asked by a UK customs official what my job was. I'm never really sure how to answer this, so I said (truthfully), "I suppose I'm a comedian."

He looked at me suspiciously, like I had inadvertently hinted at my membership in Al Qaeda.

"Oh yeah, 'ow come I've never 'eard of you?" he growled, like a Dickensian workhouse keeper.

"I don't know, maybe I'm not famous enough," I squeaked nervously.

That was true, of course, because if I were more famous, he would have heard of me. But I got the impression he thought I was mocking him for not knowing who I was; his attitude got more and more hostile, and it got especially uncomfortable when his colleague asked for a selfie with me.

The whole transaction made us both feel terrible and a little stupid. Him for looking like a jackass in front of his workmate, and me for not being more famous.

Anyway I got the heroin past the cocksucker so I suppose that's the main thing.

My point is this: people want to be famous so that they can feel special and cool, but in my experience being famous feels like the opposite of that. It usually just makes everybody around you feel a little dirty and weird. The only people who love being famous are dirty and weird to start with.

Fame is like money. You think it'll get to a level where it'll solve all of your problems, but that's bullshit. It's a chimera, a will-o'-the-wisp. If money solves all your problems, then you were a shallow, heartless dick to start with, and fame is no different.

Not that all famous people are bad. On the contrary. I interviewed hundreds of really very famous people when I hosted the late-night show and I'd say the mensch-to-douche ratio was about the same as the average bar, maybe even a bit better because most of these people were on their best behavior.

I suspect everyone, whether they admit it or not, would like to be famous. Otherwise why would Facebook and Instagram and all those *look at me* social media sites exist. It's all just ersatz *People* magazine "at home" pieces. Desperate, sad folk writing about their emotions in their blogs because no one wanted to interview them. (Jesus! Is that why I'm writing this? Current mood: horny.)

It's also a popularly held belief that famous people will be offended if you don't recognize them, which isn't really true. I don't know many famous people who think about it that much, but in order to establish dominance during interactions with famous people, the most common thing to do is to pretend you have no idea they are famous.

"I don't really watch TV but I was flipping through the channels . . ."

The implication in this statement is obvious. The person is saying they're more important and valid than watching some foreign-born clown who dances for nickels on a stupid shitshow late show. At least that's how I always took it.

I got a beauty one night in Glasgow.

I had returned to Glasgow for Christmas and had arranged to meet some old friends in a ubiquitous chip bar in the city's west end. "Ra Chip," as it's known in local parlance, is the bar I used to work in when I was a youngster. It's a great pub that sells Fürsten-berg lager on tap, which is the strongest beer I have ever encountered in my life. It's rocket fuel; even hardened Scottish drunks are powerless against its mighty blitzkrieg attack to the cerebral cortex, so consequently Ra Chip always has at least one or two spectacular examples of dipsomaniacal psychosis every night, usually toward closing time. Combine that with the fact that it was the festive season and the place was packed to the gunnels with office parties as well as the regular inebriates and you begin to get a sense of the bacchanalian atmosphere in the joint that evening. What I'm saying is that it was a terrible place for a sober alky to be. I stood by the public telephone at the far end of the bar.

> *Obviously the public telephone is more of a decoration these days, as people text each other all the time even if they are sitting at the same table, but when I worked in the bar it was at this very location where I overheard a tipsy gentleman telling his wife he'd be late home as he was in the emergency room having broken his leg. The most rudimentary visual inspection of his lower extremities, even as they were encased in slightly stained brown corduroy trousers, revealed that this was an unmitigated charade, and I have always wondered how he approached that particular detail when he finally got home.*
>
> *"They've got this new treatment, darlin', it's amazin' . . ."*

I was trying to stay as far from the action as I could, planning to get out of the bar as soon as my pals arrived.

It was then that I first saw him. Drunk Angry Scotsman.

He was looking at me from the other side of the mobbed pub. At least one of his eyes was looking at me; his other eye seemed to be scanning the room for bees. But that one eye, the steady one, was glaring at me with a hatred that I recognize from childhood. A hatred that screams, "You think yer great but yer no great. Yer shite." (Ah school!)

I'm not a hard man, and drunks, especially Glaswegian ones, can be violent and unpredictable. Since I am also Glaswegian and I speak the sign language of the saloon, I could tell this guy was contemplating causing me physical harm, but I could also tell that his confused mind was writing checks his body couldn't possibly cash in its current condition. His extreme drunkenness had rendered him about as threatening as a *TV Guide* crossword puzzle so I didn't feel intimidated. Just perplexed. Why me? Why did he hate me so much? I didn't know him, I was sure of that, and there were so many other people he could hate who were closer and more convenient. Why hate the quiet guy trying to hide by the telephone?

I didn't have to wonder too long, though. After a few minutes of seething he worked himself up to head in my direction. He stumbled past the chubby women squeezed into their bright Top Shop dresses, pushed past the chubbier men who reeked of beery lust and Axe body spray, his one good eye staying on me as the other kept a lookout for more bees. At last, after about ten minutes of struggling through the throng and nearly being thumped once or twice by other drinkers who cared little for his manner and singleness of purpose, he got to me.

He was about a foot shorter than I am, which surprised him, and his face was ruddy as a baboon's arse. He stabbed his moist, corpulent, nicotine-stained index finger into my chest and spat:

"Ah don't know who you fuckin' are!"

"Yes, you do," I said.

"Naw, ah doan't. Ah huv no fuckin' idea who you are," he growled. "An Ah've never seen yer stoopit American show oan the telly."

"Then how do you know it's *my* show you've never seen if you don't know who *I* am?"

He thought for a minute. An actual, for-real minute. Not just a literary pause. About a full sixty seconds. His good eye looking puzzled, the other one frantically searching for help. He eventually figured out his riposte.

"Shut up, ya cunt," he mumbled, and began the long, dangerous journey back to his beverage.

I liked him. I think we could have been friends if we'd met at a different time. And I understood the poor bastard too. Trapped in resentment and alcohol. I know what that feels like.

To this day, even without the alcohol, I can find myself angry at Kardashian types for their seemingly fabulous documented life even though I know it is a fictional construct and I would never want it for myself in reality anyway. Occasionally I am irritated by ridiculously green and gauche adolescent YouTube comedians who are much better at making younger people laugh than I am and wouldn't last fifteen seconds in front of a real crowd. If I meet them I might pretend that I don't know who they are even though I do.

Sometimes I find myself riddled with jealousy for contemporaries who seem to have been far luckier than me or are just more popular. Other people's fame sometimes makes me feel like I have failed. Whenever I watch awards shows from Hollywood on television, I feel like I'm being excluded even though I always turn down any invitation to attend or even host them.

Luckily I have found a cure for my unpleasant distaste for the success of others. Here it is:

If you want to not suffer from jealousy of colleagues who seem to be doing well or to not be angry at famous people like Kardashians or Hiltons or whoever the hell it is burning up the media by the time you read this, then be happy for them.

Wish them well.

It will set you free.

18

A Marked Man

I blame Constantine the Great, the Tudors, and Ally MacLeod for my ambivalence toward team sports. Constantine for his cynical appropriation of Christianity into the Roman Empire, making it the biggest megachurch in history, so that by medieval times everyone in Europe had wildly different interpretations of the garbled doctrine of this wildly popular brand of superstitious nonsense. This in time led to the Reformation, which was badly handled by Henry Tudor—Henry VIII—who, although better remembered as a chubby, insane tyrant and wife killer, was the incompetent inbred buffoon whose policy in Ireland kicked off the sectarian troubles that have plagued that unhappy land ever since.

Ireland is very close to Scotland, not just geographically but culturally and emotionally. As I've mentioned, that's particularly true of Glasgow, which has a huge Irish population. When I was growing up, the sectarian hatred between Catholics and Protestants that was popping off explosively in Northern Ireland was also hot in Glasgow, and each side had a soccer team—Glasgow Celtic for the Catholics and Glasgow Rangers for the Protestants. Celtic wore green and Rangers wore blue, and their followers did the same, which made for a quick and efficient way for young men to locate, identify, and beat the shit out of each other. I'm told it's different now, but I learned as a kid to associate team sports with the threat of a good kicking, so naturally I tried to keep my involvement to a minimum.

The Scottish national soccer team offers an escape from this unpleasantness. It has a unifying effect by co-opting both factions into the "Tartan Army"—the affectionate name given to the wildly enthusiastic fans who follow the team to whatever exotic or obscure international location they are playing and boisterously sing drunken support and encouragement no matter how woeful the performance.

> *The wonderfully laconic and crumpled English comedian Arthur Smith once observed that although the Scottish national side contained hugely talented players of outstanding ability and renown, their results as a team were terrible, or as he put it, "Scotland—great on paper. Shit on grass."*

In 1978 there was a miracle. I was sixteen years old and Scotland qualified for the FIFA World Cup finals tournament to take place in Argentina. It is hard to express the level of hysteria that this produced in Scotland at the time. Not only had we qualified to take part in the competition, but England—the *Auld Enemy* who had actually won the trophy in 1966—had not. Scottish people were literally—and I'm not kidding—dancing in the streets.

If the Independence referendum had been held then, the UK would have been dissolved immediately.

A level of hysteria and delusion bewitched the populace the likes, of which would not be seen again in Britain until many years later when, the day after the tragic death of Diana Spencer, everyone convinced themselves they had always loved the "people's princess," and hadn't been baying for her blood twenty-four hours earlier for fucking a coked-up Arab. It was hard not to get caught up in the hurricane of sentimentality over the World Cup qualification, and I was no exception. Ally MacLeod, the Scottish manager of the team, had me and many others convinced that Scotland, who were wild outsiders in the tournament, could actually win this thing. We called the team and ourselves "Ally's Army." This was our *destiny*; the world was about to see the wonder of our greatness. There was even a chart-topping song:

> *We're on the march with Ally's Army,*
> *We're going to the Argentine*
> *And we'll really shake them up when we win the*
>   *World Cup*
> *'Cause Scotland are the greatest football team!*

In the first two games of the tournament, Scotland played pretty badly and found themselves in the horrible position of having to win by two clear goals in the third game in order to advance to the next round. Dejection took hold because the third game was against the Netherlands, which was generally agreed to be one of the best teams in the world at the time. Unbelievably Scotland took the lead and in the sixty-eighth minute scored the required second goal. It was a moment which many Scottish people, even ones who weren't born at the time, have branded into their psyche: Archie's run.

Archie Gemmill took the ball past two world-class defenders

and put Scotland ahead with what is still agreed to be one of the greatest moments in World Cup football. This goal is famous beyond the sport itself. It's featured as a plot point in the movie *Trainspotting*. It is a Mona Lisa of a goal. If this goal were a woman, it would be thirty-year-old Marilyn Monroe; if it were a man, it would be John Lennon at twenty. It was spectacular and breathtaking and full of hope and beauty and for a shimmering golden moment Scotland really was the greatest footballing nation on earth. Three minutes later Johnny Rep—the son of a bitch even had a rock star name—scored for the Netherlands and, if you forgive a moment of local-newspaper-style sports writing, the plucky Scots were crushed under the merciless cleated Dutch clog of despair.

For many of my contemporaries and indeed for me this was our first experience with heartbreak. I'm still mad about it.

We didn't win. We didn't shake them up, we didn't win the World Cup, and we weren't the greatest football team. It was devastating. The frustration was so visceral, so distressing that I think it ruined me as a fan. I can still appreciate athleticism and prowess and skill, but never again will I give my heart to a bunch of young men in matching sportswear. Well maybe if One Direction reunite for a Nike commercial.

Given my disinterest in team sports, it's surprising how often I seem to attend sporting events. Perhaps that's explained by America's love of competition. America loves sports. Especially corporate America. If you work for a big broadcast company like CBS or ABC or SiriusXM, then you are in the employ of the Corporate Monster and in the interests of your continued employment you will have to deal with, cooperate with, and, every now and again, socialize with entertainment executives. By entertainment executives I mean not only the accountants and number crunchers at the networks themselves, but lawyers and agents and managers. These are men and women who have convinced themselves that they are artistic in some way rather than just Wall Street goons. They deeply want to believe that they give a shit about something other than money. They don't, of course, but sports makes them feel that they do. Actually I think I'm being unfair—it's not just entertainment executives, it's all corporate executives. There are exceptions, of course; there are the interesting corporate figures who are strange and mercurial and follow the beat of their own drum, but they are in the minority and tend to live on the edges of the game. They tend to be either wildly successful or wildly not. Like artists, I suppose.

To this end I found myself in Florida in February 2007 for the Super Bowl. A battle for the ages. (Again. Happens every fucking year!) This year the frisky Indianapolis Colts battled the ferocious Chicago Bears in the stadium owned by the mighty Miami Dolphins. (To be honest I struggled here with an adjective for the Dolphins but it didn't seem right to say "slimy" or "fishy-smelling," so I just went with the generic sports "mighty.")

> *Sports teams in the United States almost always have names which help create Roman forum levels of excitement around the contests. Bears versus Eagles, or Jaguars fighting Cowboys, or Mavericks battling Bulls. There are exceptions, of course—Penguins versus Ducks sounds more adorable than thrilling, and Packers against Broncos could be a gay porn website. I admit that actual Senators against actual Panthers is a match that I think most people would want to see.*

CBS was televising the event and required my presence as a member of their cavalcade of stars, along with the chiseled actors from their crime dramas and the grumpy fat comedians and nervous pecky actresses from their sitcoms. I was horribly uncomfortable amongst the cargo shorts and shouty pseudo-locker-room environment of pretend friendliness, but I had to be there. I was part of the CBS *family*. Corporations like to use the word *family* to imply a sense of bonding amongst their employees. I don't understand this. Most people I know have extremely mixed and complicated feelings about their families. Maybe that's just the people I know.

My discomfort at being involved in the event was somewhat tempered by being, for the first time in my life, in the sparkling city of Miami. The fact that this sexy, humid, vibrant, artistic Latin city can exist in the same nation as say, Bismarck, North Dakota, is a testament to the wild diversity of America. I suppose that explains at least partially why America struggles so much with itself culturally. (I mean no disrespect to Bismarck, it's a nice, quiet, friendly town in my experience, just very different from Miami.)

Even in February Miami felt hot and humid and I felt weird and isolated amongst the shiny-faced sports cult. I loved doing the late-night show, but I was beginning to suspect that I was much more of an outsider in the broadcast television world than even the most vitriolic or observant critics had pointed out. I was also struggling with the fact that it had already been a year since my father had died. All of this created perfect atmospheric conditions for my first tattoo.

People get tattoos for all sorts of reasons. They were drunk, they fell in love, they fell out of love, they love a pet, or their kids, or their country, or their mom. They get tattoos to help them remember or they get tattoos they wish they could forget. They get them to set themselves apart from people who do not have tattoos, or they get them to be part of a gang that does. There are as many different reasons to get a tattoo as there are people with tattoos. Or even more, since I didn't get all of mine for the same reasons. Actually when I get one now I don't even need to have a reason. I just see a boring piece of aging white flesh on my body and think, "I could hang a picture there." There is only one reason I can think of that would never inspire me to get a tattoo: your approval.

You have my permission, not that you need it, to dislike my tattoos, or even the fact that I have them. But you do not have permission to transcend the bounds of normal societal politeness just because I have ink. For example, I would never approach a stranger who had made the decision to wear bright orange nylon sweatpants and comment on them. I would never remark on another person's choice of haircut. This is because I try very hard not to be a dick.

> It's not just tattoos, there are other situations that seem to encourage dickiness in others. Pregnant women have to swat off hands that feel entitled to touch their bellies. In fact, I suppose women, pregnant or not, have to swat off hands that feel entitled to touch them, but that's a whole deeper level of dickitude.

What I'm saying is please don't tell me that the tattoos will look like shit when I'm an old man. They won't. I might look like shit myself, but I can have the tattoos refreshed. Also, mind your own fucking business. And if you *do* have tattoos, then I hope you like them but it doesn't mean we are on the same team or in a gang or family.

"Hey! You wear pants! So do I!"

It would seem I'm a bit touchy and defensive, maybe even *adolescent* about this and I think that's probably true. My apologies, I was being a dick.

I think it's because I don't really know why I have tattoos, but it feels like I should.

The Family Crest

I loved my father very much. It was not a complicated relationship; it got a little rocky when I was a teenager, but that's as it should be. We had an easy quietness about us by the time he died. He knew that I adored him and I know that he felt the same about me. I miss him and I wish he were still around. He hated tattoos, said they made a man look like a criminal. Mind you, he also said if a woman smoked a cigarette outside she was a prostitute. I loved my dad but I rarely agreed with him. It struck me, about a year after his death, that I could get a tattoo in memory of him and which seemed ironic, appropriate, and respectful at the same time.

The Ferguson name is an old and very noble one, although I suspect my branch of the family came by it by being serfs on Ferguson land at some point in the grim and distant past. There is a family crest—a bee alighting on a Scots thistle—and the motto is *Dulcius ex Aspiris.* Sweeter after difficulty. My father was very proud of the name and the motto, so it seemed a perfect choice.

This first tattoo was placed on my right shoulder by the owner of the Miami Ink parlor, Ami James, an ex–Israeli army sniper who uses his remarkably steady hand for more benign pursuits these days.

My mother was touched and a little scandalized by the tattoo. She clucked and shook her head as she had often done when I was younger, but I think she really rather liked it. But just to be safe, I never got another until after her death three years later, when I was marked with . . .

The Other Family Crest

I had not planned on getting more than one tattoo, but about a year after my mother had died I began to hear her voice—not literally but in that odd way that the dead can live on in dreams and musings. She seemed to be saying (in classic Mrs. Doubtfire tones), "Oh, you get a tattoo for your father but your poor old mother gets nothing, eh?"

I called the Shamrock tattoo parlor on the Sunset Strip in LA and made an appointment.

My mother's maiden name was Ingram, also an old Scottish name probably bestowed on her family the same way my Fergusons got theirs. There's also a crest but it's very ornate and heraldic and I didn't want to look like a souvenir tea towel from Edinburgh castle, so I settled on a Celtic cross on my left shoulder with the Ingram motto written underneath. *Magnanimus Esto.* Basically "think big," I suppose.

The tattoo I got for my father was painless and quick and hassle free. The one I got for my mother was agony and took a long time before it felt okay, which mirrors my relationship with her. Perhaps that's unfair. My mother's tattoo took longer because I added another one at the same time. I had picked up from someone along the way that having an even number of tattoos was unlucky, and given my susceptibility to OCD and magical thinking, I decided to get . . .

Join or Die!

Placed on my right forearm. This copy of the famous dramatic and iconic cartoon Benjamin Franklin drew for the *Pennsylvania Gazette* in 1754 seemed a fitting choice, as I'd recently become an American citizen. Plus, it looks cool and by then the strange addiction to the process of being tattooed began to sink in.

> Later on I would actually do a show for the History Channel called Join or Die in which I'd use the old talk show format to have discussions about history. It wasn't a bad idea but a little overproduced. Had the show continued I would have dropped much of the structure and concentrated on the fun and spontaneity of the discussion, but it suffered at the hands of nervous midlevel cargo-short executives who had pushed for the fussy format in the first place. I said going in, and I believe this to be true, that in order to figure out a talk show you need to be bold, make at least 100 episodes, run it every night, and find out what works and what doesn't. This sounds like a ridiculously flamboyant way to go about things, but it isn't really. These shows are relatively cheap to produce, especially when you

have a minimal writing team, and they're quick to make a profit. Unfortunately, this goes against pussy corporate thinking, which always, and I mean always, says, "Let's do one a week and see how it goes."

That can work for tightly scripted, topical, political shows like John Oliver's or Samantha Bee's but will rarely if ever be successful in the talk realm. This is why the big network shows are kept running and the hosts replaced as they go mad or die off and why the Brits, to their utter frustration, find it impossible to make a long-running late-night show. They always approach it too timidly or wuss out before they have worn the audience into making the show a habit. When I began in late night the show failed for about 100 episodes (and often after that) but I was shielded by the massive testicles of David Letterman, who didn't give a rat's ass about ratings or reviews. I doubt that situation would ever happen again and is one of the reasons why I would be unlikely to ever return to the game.

Megan, Milo, and Liam

By the time 2013 had rolled around I found myself back at another fucking Super Bowl, though luckily it was in another spectacular city, New Orleans. CBS had the right to broadcast the game this year and required my presence to do a week of shows in the lead-up to it.

I had been there once before, a week before the ministrations of wicked witch Katrina, and I was struck by the ancient pagan feel of the place. New Orleans doesn't feel like any other American city I've been to. It has an atmosphere more like Rome or Istanbul. A sense of the veil being very thin between this world and the worlds of the fictional and the dead. It is an eerie, haunted, and sometimes dangerous place, as any port should be.

By now I could see the light at the end of my late-night contract, and though I really did love making the show, it really was time to be free. I felt impatient and rebellious. One afternoon I sat in the lobby of the Roosevelt Hotel listening to the Talking Heads song "Drugs" in my earbuds and watching the excited, porcine, cargo-shorted, sportily-hatted TV and advertising executives who were pouring into town for yet another "battle of the ages." They were high-fiving each other and back-slapping and I even saw a couple of chest bumps.

I wanted to feel distance from them.

I felt the need for the pain of the needle.

During a commercial break in the taping of the show that night, I asked a heavily tattooed member of the studio audience for the name of a good parlor in town and was directed to Electric Ladyland on Frenchmen St.

After the show I headed there with Tuyen and Lisa, the gorgeous women who worked as the hair and makeup team on the show and who occasionally danced with me on the stage; my assistant, Phil; and Rebecca, who was head of my production company at the time. They had all decided, for their own reasons, which it's not my place to talk about, to get tattoos, so we made a night of it. Dinner and tats—how very sophisticated.

Of course I had to get two to keep an odd number, so I decided on a banner with the names of my children for my right arm and an endless Celtic knot with the date I married Megan in its center for my left. I wanted more than just dead people's names and slogans on my body, so this seemed right. Also tattoos are permanent so I needed something eternal. My children will always be my children and Megan will always be my wife.

Ed Dieringer is the owner of Electric Ladyland, which is as fine a tattoo parlor as has ever been my good fortune to visit. Walls covered in imagery, good music, and a crew of artists who are satisfyingly dyed and pierced and darkly clad and slightly scary-looking even though they are friendly and funny. The minute you step into the place you are, by association, a little bit more cool.

Ed designed my tats and then put them on, which takes a little while, so we got to talking. He complimented me on being one of the first showbiz people he had met who wasn't an asshole, which I was very honored to hear. I found out from him that he had been a cop in the NOPD until Katrina, the aftermath of which had given him some terrible things to see and deal with. He told me he was much happier doing what he was doing now and I envied his clarity of thought, although I did not envy how it came to him. Katrina was, I believe, America's Chernobyl. A dangerous portent of a crumbling infrastructure and the ending of the myth of invincibility.

One Less of Them . . .

Billy Connolly tells a story that I love which is pertinent to my desire to be marked with ink. When he was fifty he decided to get rings through his nipples (this is not for me). As the job was done, in a tattoo parlor no doubt, he heard his piercer say, "One less of them, one more of us."

I continue to be tattooed. I met the amazingly talented Samantha Mancino and have donated my flesh to her dark art. To date I have suns and moons and crows and constellations and a compass rose and a Viking ship held above a sea monster by a hot-air balloon. By the time you read this there will be more. I can't tell you what they'll be because I don't know myself. I no longer know if there is an odd number or an even number, because they have all begun to run into each other. Hard to say where one ends and another begins, but each time I flinch from the artist's sting I feel a little less one of them and a little more one of me.

19

Japanese Bar Mitzvah

When I first visited the United States in 1975 at the age of thirteen, it had such a profound effect on me that it has influenced everything I have done since. The aforementioned Steve McQueen of my family, my uncle James, had immigrated to Long Island from Scotland in the early 1960s, working his own passage across the Atlantic on a tramp steamer, which sounds a lot more sexually deviant than it actually was. My aunt Susan joined him shortly afterward with their two young children, and their next two kids were born in the US.

It was the great glamour story of my childhood, that we were related to Americans, and it was a point of honor for me in the school playground after the moon landings in 1969, when I was seven. Cliffy Bell, the best fighter in my elementary class and a budding local celebrity thug, even invited me to his house, where his rather intimidating, whisky-soaked Hogarthian parents grilled me about what I had heard of America. They were enthusiastic participants in Glasgow's Grand Ole Opry, a society that still meets in Glasgow today to enjoy line dancing, country and western music, and dressing like extras from politically incorrect Western movies of the 1950s. Did my uncle know Johnny Cash?

An odd but, I'm assured, common phenomenon of the aging
process is that childhood memories long thought to be for-
gotten seem to resurface with shocking and vivid clarity. I
am unsure whether to believe in the verisimilitude of these
recollections or whether they are just one of the entertain-
ments of a decaying brain.

America seemed very far away then; transatlantic travel was
expensive and belonged to the swinging sixties jet set, well out of
the reach of working-class families. So the only contact I had with
my American cousins was through short and taciturn letters that
I later found out they had been forced to write by their parents. I
loved these letters, though, not only for their content, which was
full of exotic references to things like "drugstores" and "bowling"
but because of how they looked and felt.

They were sent in official-looking envelopes that had *par avion*
written on them and were bordered with little flags that made it
look like you were receiving correspondence from a spy. They were
written on "air mail" paper, which was a cool, sophisticated dark
blue color and light and thin as a Bible page. They reeked of an
international James Bond existence full of glamour and sultry foreign women in tight Chanel two-piece suits who wore kohl and
lipstick and had pens that turned into machine guns. I later
learned that Long Island was not in fact a hotbed of sexy Cold War
espionage, but if you had told me that then I would never have
believed or forgiven you.

American cultural imperialism was at its most thrilling,
caffeine-fueled, Coca-Cola, Saturn V peak in the late sixties and
early seventies, and that coupled with the legend of the American

Fergusons had left me convinced that the United States was paradise, a magical wonderland where it wasn't dark all day in the winter, it never rained, you didn't have to eat fucking potatoes if you didn't want to, and fat, grumpy old ladies didn't belt you every day when you got to school.

My standards for paradise were much the same then as they are now.

Freddie Laker, a UK businessman, was the first person to implement cheap air travel from Britain to the US. Given that my older siblings had recently been allowed to go on subsidized school trips to Spain and the Soviet Union (I know!) in the previous couple of years, and my little sister was not yet entitled to the one foreign voyage allocated per childhood in my family, it was my luck to accompany my father on a super-economy trip on a Laker Airways DC-10 from Prestwick, Scotland, to NYC and back for the two weeks that surrounded my thirteenth birthday.

I have written and talked a lot about that vacation, and I won't meander on about it again here—I'm not quite at that point in the aging process yet—but because the trip was so profound to me, it gave me an idea for my own children.

My eldest son Milo's biological mother is Jewish, which in the Jewish tradition makes him a Jew too. I don't think it's any secret that I am not Jewish, but I wanted to honor that part of his heritage when he reached the age for Bar Mitzvah by offering him a trip in the spirit of what my own father had done for me, just the two of us, to anywhere he wanted to go in the world. I'll do the same for my younger boy, Liam, when he reaches that age too. Liam is not Jewish, but a precedent has been set.

Since he was a baby, Milo has loved cartoons, as all children seem to, but as he got older this love turned into an enthusiasm and a passion for animation as an art form. He loves all forms, from the giant Disney and DreamWorks epics (look out for *How to Train Your Dragon 3*—coming soon to a theater near you!) to experimental abstract stuff which leaves me feeling like I'm watching something in a different language and perhaps from a different planet. A particular enthusiasm of his is anime, the wildly popular Japanese school of animation. I've watched some of it to be supportive, and from what I can tell it contains a lot of evil villains, poetic heroes, tough and impossibly large-breasted women, cute comedy creatures, and a great deal of noisy combat. Perfect for a teenage boy. I can see why he's into it.

Also like many of his generation, Milo loves video games from Mario Kart to Minecraft and all points in between, so it was not a total surprise that he chose Japan for his Mitzvah trip.

I had never really thought of visiting Japan before, so I wasn't for it and I wasn't against it. I'd just never really thought about it—like having sex with a ginger person—it just never really came up.

But I was wrong, so wrong, to not think about going to Japan. Japan is amazing, incredible, wild fantastic, and so different. I loved it. If I had gone there as a younger man I'm sure I would have stayed and you would have been reading this vertically down the page right now.

From the moment we arrived at Narita International Airport I felt we were really somewhere else. This is an experience that gets more and more challenging as corporations take over the globe and the Borg becomes all-powerful. "Wow, their Olive Garden/ Starbucks/Apple Store is so different from ours."

Most of the time now, travel now feels a bit like aging to me—everywhere looks kind of the same but they've changed it in subtle ways that leave me feeling unsettled and a little vulnerable. I like old-school travel, which involved big, dramatic visual clues that let you know these people have a history and a society which is cognizant but independent from yours. You're not the only game in town, fucker!

> *I think this is very good for you, gives you a sense of humility and place. I first became aware of this sensation in my early twenties when I worked on a construction site in Hurlem. One morning on the way to my job I noticed I was the only white person on a busy NYC bus. I was brought up in the Scottish town of Cumbernauld in the 1970s, which I'm guessing had a population then of about 99.5 percent Caucasian, so this is not something that happens much to white guys there. I didn't feel intimidated and I don't know if anyone else on the bus thought about it, but I have noticed that people who purposely step outside their own ethnic group in some way have got a better chance of escaping that most loathsome and destructive manifestation of fear: racism. It's not a guarantee, of course, but it's a start.*

It dawned on me as we rode in the ridiculously clean taxi from the Tokyo airport to the hotel that I had not taken a trip for the sole purpose of a vacation in perhaps a decade or more. Every time I went somewhere, there was a job to do or a show to be on. This was different; my only job was to experience the journey with my boy. It felt terrific, even though I'd been rendered numb with fatigue from the seemingly endless flight from LA.

Time will tell what the experience of the trip will be like for Milo; he has his own journey and his own decisions to make, but for me it was something of a satori—a kick in the eye. I had been entrenched in LA show business in a very real way since *The Drew Carey Show* in 1995, and with ten years of the late-night show under my belt, I had almost forgotten there was a world outside of ratings and gossip and schadenfreude and money. We had the greatest time!

We went to Robot Restaurant in downtown Tokyo, which is perhaps best described as a hybrid of *Blade Runner* and Medieval Times (the theme restaurant, not the era). The patrons or guests or audience, I'm not really sure what we were, sit on either side of an auditorium and are served food by impossibly attractive young women. I can't remember what the food was or how it tasted, because that's not really what you are there for. You are there for the show, which, to the best of my knowledge—and I could be getting the plot horribly wrong here—is an epic battle between two giant robot armies that are controlled by an amazing team of gloriously fit Japanese women in metal bikinis and oiled-up young men playing giant drums. The whole thing has an Asian metal soundtrack that is played at the volume of the Rolls-Royce RB211 jet engine in full-thrust phase. It is as awesome and thrilling as it sounds. Even better.

Milo and I were both teenage boys for that meal.

We went to Nara, the ancient capital of imperial Japan, to the enormous Buddhist temple which sits in gardens that are so tranquil and picturesque that they make you feel a little weepy. It was here we met dozens of little Japanese kids who were on a school trip. They all wanted to practice their English, so we (obviously not being from around these parts) were asked countless times and in the cutest way possible, "How are you today?"

When answered by a middle-aged Scotsman, "I'm fine, how are you?" seems to be the funniest thing imaginable to any Japanese person under the age of seven. If I lived there I'd make a fortune; apparently I'm a hybrid of SpongeBob and Shrek.

The deer that roam the temple garden in Nara are much loved by the locals—I don't know if I'd use the word *sacred* but they are certainly given a lot of leeway. I have to say they were the only rude Japanese I encountered on the entire trip. For a few yen you can buy some treats to feed them, and of course everyone does and the deer expect it, but when Milo had finished handing out the supplies he had purchased, the deer didn't believe him and tried to nuzzle their way into his trousers to check for more. This began an encounter which was one of the funniest physical comedy routines I've ever witnessed as the gangly American teenager and the Japanese royal deer tussled over the grazing rights to the young man's pockets.

We stayed in a traditional Japanese hotel in Kyoto where I was asked to wear a "swimming shirt"—a skintight sweatshirt thingy, not so flattering—at the pool to cover up my tattoos. The only people who have tattoos in Japan—or certainly the only Japanese patrons of this hotel who had tattoos—are gangsters, and they didn't want me upsetting the other guests with my possible involvement in organized crime. I was happy to comply; it made me feel badass, which is not something I experience often anymore.

In the hotel we slept on traditional Japanese beds. I was worried about how comfortable I was going to be sleeping on a mat on the floor with a block of wood for a pillow. I wondered if I'd get flashbacks to nights spent in Stuart St. police station in Glasgow during the drinking days, but I was shocked at how deeply I slept. Really, I still don't understand it. Milo and I had beds, or mats I suppose, that were right next to each other. One night, he got up to go to the bathroom; still half asleep, he accidentally stepped on my face and even then, being stomped by a hairy size 13 foot, I still knew I wasn't in jail and was able to go back to sleep.

He's older now, so if we do this again he can have his own room.

A highlight of the trip was a guided meditation by a Buddhist monk in a temple in Kyoto. The setting was perfect. Bamboo mats, wooden temple, and a Zen garden complete with bonsai trees and little tinkly fountains that always make me want to pee. Our monk, who was chubby and ageless and spectacularly monkish in his appearance, with bald head and thick Dalai Lama glasses and a saffron robe, spoke absolutely no English, so we had to communicate through an interpreter, a charming mumsy woman from Tokyo called Kaori whose English, if I'm honest, was a bit better than my own. Kaori was a good sport and joined in for our half hour of meditation. We sat criss-cross applesauce on the mats, our hands forming little bridges in our laps, and the monk, through Kaori, told us to focus on a thing in front of us. A plant from the garden perhaps, or a tree, something within our direct field of vision. We were instructed to follow along in his breathing, which we did. He set a little timer and off we went. Every now and then he would bang a little gong and the resonance of the sound would drift for longer and longer stretches in my mind. It was wonderfully calm, although after a while my old joints started screaming in their quiet way that perhaps it was time to get up before I was no longer able. By the end of the thirty minutes I was very glad to be standing and made all the old man noises that the occasion demanded. Groaning and sighing and stretching like an old wooden boat being hauled into dry dock. The monk grumbled something to Kaori and she laughed and I felt ashamed.

Afterward when we had been dismissed I asked her what he had said; she told me that he feels all the same things in his body getting up from a meditation, he just doesn't make so much bloody noise about it. So it turns out, in this instance at least, my shame was well placed.

We went to "the best sushi restaurant in the world," as made famous in the award-winning documentary film *Jiro Dreams of Sushi*. The film looks at the life of the great master chef Jiro and his equally impressive sons who are continuing his tradition of excellence. It's a delightful and inspiring movie, and Milo and I both watched and loved it in anticipation of the trip. The meal was indeed extraordinary, in part because it was prepared and served by the people who you feel you've gotten to know from the film.

The restaurant itself—the only sushi restaurant to receive two Michelin stars—is a small, unremarkable-looking diner-type joint in a Tokyo subway station. It was hugely expensive and very formal and the sushi was spectacular, although I'm not sure if I know the difference between good sushi and great sushi or even good sushi and okay sushi (everybody can tell what bad sushi is, if not at the time of ingesting then certainly within a few hours).

Interestingly, although I loved it before, I have not eaten or had the desire to eat sushi since this meal and actually have since become vegan. I guess when you go out, go out with a bang.

Speaking of which . . . *the bathrooms.*

When Japanese people visit the West for the first time, they must think we are backward heathen medieval savages based on our toilets alone. And they might be right. Without getting too graphic about the art of poopery, I have to say that our Western approach to the follow-up operations after number twos are not perhaps up to speed with other lessons learned in personal hygiene in the centuries since the Black Death.

If, for example—and I wouldn't wish this on you unless it was something you wanted and participated in with another consenting adult—you inadvertently got some poop, some human feces, some man dung on your hand or arm or face, would it be sufficient for you to wipe off said ass fruit with a piece of soft, dry paper, wash your hands, and chalk the whole thing up to experience?

No, of course it wouldn't!

You'd want hot water and soap and towels and more soap and some sanitizer and maybe the kind understanding counsel of an old friend. Why then is it okay for us to drop, wipe, and walk? It is not enough, I say. Not nearly enough.

The Japanese are sublimely and impressively aware of this. Any of you who have had the luxury of executing a humpty in the Land of the Rising Sun will know what I mean.

My first time in a Japanese bathroom was a life changer.

You enter the cubicle and the lights change. They become moody and dim, like something big is about to happen.

Like something intense is going down.

Which with any luck it is.

The toilet lid opens automatically as if welcoming you to a ride, a ride to another dimension. Nervously you drop your pants and sit on the cushioned seat, which is *warmed*!

Warmed! And by electricity, not by the fat guy who used the stall before you at the airport.

You conduct the business which cannot be named, and you think to yourself, "Well, that was nice," or you cry or sing or whatever it is you normally do and you think that it's over.

But it's not over, it's just about to begin.

First come the water jets pushing and throbbing, scooting from some hidden hose beneath your nether regions; these temperate jets, aimed by discreet robots, hose your portal of doom and sandblast away any residual entourage left over from the main event. It is transcendental. It's euphoric. It is as if the fountain display outside the Bellagio in Las Vegas has been transferred to your anus.

You think, "Wow that was nice, it can't get better than that!" but you are wrong. It can get better than that.

Then the dryers start. Dryers! A balmy mistral, a soothing trade wind to dry the now scrupulously clean landscape. When they finally, sadly, stop, you think, "That was unbelievable, there is no way it can get better than that!"

But you are wrong again!

When the wind stops—POOF!—a shot of scented talcum powder right in the tiger's eye.

It is not often I say this, but I left that bathroom a better man than when I walked in. When it was all over I thought the same thought I had on the airplane as it left Japan.

I wonder how soon I can go back.

20

Morning at LAX

I moved to Los Angeles from London in January 1995, which was a thunderously stupid career choice in the short term. But in the long term, with the exception of a few rather embarrassing decisions and performances, I think things have turned out okay.

I had been sober for nearly three years and had finally begun to make some inroads on fixing the mess that my drinking had left me in professionally. I had performed a lot of stand-up comedy in the UK and acted in a lot of theater when I was drinking. Through the lens of self-delusion so thoughtfully provided by active alcoholism, I was firmly convinced of my own genius. Unfortunately, the rest of the world was less sure. That was particularly true in London, where I'd disappointed more than just friends and lovers.

It wasn't that I was *always* drunk or hungover on stage; sometimes I was on my game and could do the job, but too many times I just couldn't. I was what could charitably be described as inconsistent. Now inconstancy is not necessarily a huge problem for an artist who has a large legacy of successful work in their wake, but for someone who is starting out it can be a real handicap. The fact that I was unreliable and a dick had understandably made television executives and theater and movie producers wary of including me in their endeavors. But after I'd had a couple of years of sobriety, people were beginning to believe that I might be capable of actually delivering good or at least acceptable work—not to mention turning up on time and not being a horse's arse whenever difficulties arose in productions, as they inevitably do.

In short, my British career finally looked like it might be heading somewhere. If I had stayed, I like to think that I'd have done well as a presenter of some whimsical documentary series about badgers or history on the BBC, or played an eccentric but brilliant detective in a beloved and long-running TV series which would ultimately have led, after many awards along the way, to a knighthood and my own celebrity cookbook.

However, I was young and impatient and greedy and full of resentment against an establishment that was not as forgiving and welcoming as I believed they should be given my newly pious life. I thought if I moved to LA I would speed up the process of my professional rehabilitation. I would succeed in America and that would show those bastards in charge of the BBC their folly in not lauding me when they had the chance. I cringe now at the utter asshattery of my arrogance at that time, but on the upside it helps me be more understanding of younger performers whose behavior seems less than rational.

Truth is, I was terrified I would fail. That I'd be a failure, a loser, another desperate, bitter wannabe. I hadn't really defined what success would look like—vague notions of global acclaim coupled with an early but glamorous death that would secure my legend, something messianic like that. Nothing too grand.

I don't know why I was so afraid of failure; the most interesting people I know have failed more than they have succeeded. This may be because life is not as simple as it appears to a desperately ambitious young man, or it could be that all my friends are losers. I genuinely don't care about all that anymore, which is an enormous relief and one of the many benefits of aging.

Looking back, I think my fear of failure was not fear at all. It was shame. I felt that I was never cool enough, never thin enough, never interesting enough. I had a persistent and nagging feeling that I was an embarrassment. To whom, I'm not sure. Maybe to the aloof demon who sat on my shoulder guffawing at my sweaty attempts at validation. I suspected that everyone who had said anything negative about me was right. A bad review in the Glasgow *Evening Times* would render me almost suicidal. I am extremely thankful that I came of age before the Internet and social media, where the filthy sewage of doubt, derision, and contempt is plumbed directly into your phone every time you click on the comments (which you should never ever do).

I once confronted a journalist who wrote for the Evening Times *in Glasgow about a blistering and unfair review he had given a show of mine. I felt that not liking the performance was his prerogative, but voicing his own personal dislike of me—insulting me for who I was, what I looked like, how my voice sounded—was unnecessary and cruel. It not only rendered the review invalid but made him, to use the phrase I employed at the time of meeting him, "a miserable, shitty, mean-spirited cunt."*

He seemed genuinely mystified by my outrage and in his defense he told me, "If you stick your head above the parapet, Craig, you should expect to get shot at."

Until that moment I had not considered the notion that some people consider a performer they don't like as being an affront to them personally. Entertainment as an act of war. A parapet, for fuck's sake!

These people are idiots and should be avoided. Thankfully, though, they are not in the majority.

The twenty-plus years I have been in Los Angeles have been good to me, but the achievements that give me the most joy are familial and personal and have very little to do with professional success. I don't know if I would be capable of thinking that if I had never achieved a decent level of professional success, but I hope that sooner or later I would have come to the same understanding: it's love that counts. Relish it when you can because the time flies in a way which, although warned by countless poets and philosophers, I find myself genuinely astonished by.

Case in point. Three days ago I find myself sitting in my car in parking lot 7 opposite the United terminal at LAX. The car is a newish Range Rover. It is a spectacularly comfortable triumph of British engineering. It's a rich man's car. It's my car.

Next to me, even more taciturn than usual given his lack of sleep, is my beloved fifteen-year-old son. We have been through a lot together. I was there the day he was born, I moved into a bachelor pad with him when I got divorced from his mother when he was two years old, and I have attended countless recitals and shows and parent-teacher meetings and animated movies. When he was seven years old he was the best man at my wedding to the stepmother he adores and relies on and doesn't remember being without. He was in the hospital (but not the room) when his little brother was born. We have been all over the world together, we have been buddies and confederates since day one. But this time it's different.

This time I don't get to go.

We are at the airport so that I can drop him off with the rest of the school group he is traveling with. They are headed to Beijing and Shanghai on an educational trip. He's learning Mandarin, and I'm told he's pretty good too. He's going to try it out on the locals.

His childhood is different from mine. I'm happy about that, but I worry about him. Not about drugs or booze or stupid behavior, because he's smart and sane and knows what he wants to do with his life. He's not afraid of the world like I was, but I worry about him all the same. What about the plane? Or terrorists? What if things go crazy while he's there? I run through any number of horrifying imaginings that any parent is familiar with.

It's dark and I'm tired and he's tired and as usual we are fifteen minutes early—my father always told me, "If you're not fifteen minutes early, you're late," and I believe that to be true.

We sit in the car not talking, but I know he's excited because he hasn't been able to think about anything but this trip for weeks. I don't feel much like talking anyway. It is really fucking early.

I look around the airport and it slowly dawns on me that it has changed. Airlines I used to fly, like Continental and TWA, are gone, gobbled up by the other giants United and American. The redcaps are gone; the cops are no longer in the sleek Ford Crown Vics that always made me feel like I was in a network detective show. They are now driving paramilitary-looking SUV-type vehicles that make me feel I'm about to be in a news report. This has had an effect on the cops too. They used to have a cool swagger and a streetwise vibe; now they look and act like infantrymen in hostile territory. Maybe they're more afraid than they used to be, and I don't blame them. They have phones; they're pummeled by the same propaganda as everyone else.

Bad people are everywhere and are trying to kill us.

I wish I could keep my son at home. Keep him safe. But he is embarking on a trip that seems pivotal. He's been on school trips before, of course, and he's certainly no stranger to air travel, but this time he is headed to a world where he speaks the language and I don't. Where he is cognizant of the rules and manners and I am not. A location where he can function independently whereas I would be vulnerable and afraid and rely completely on others to guide me.

China is a very big place, but not as big as the future.

21

Draining the Swamp

Bob Rifkin is a spectacular artist. The genre which he inhabits is an often painful and unsettling one, but almost always it leaves people feeling better. Bob is a dentist both respected and revered not only among his peers but in Hollywood at large. He has renovated and restored some of the most famous grins and grimaces in the world. Movie stars and producers and comedians and singers and lawyers and agents and just the regular rich and vain clamber over themselves to be sculpted by his drill. A good smile is essential in a town where everyone is wearing sunglasses all the time because of the glare and the lying. Among the spiritually disenfranchised, yoga-phony, pompous smugfuckery of Los Angeles the teeth are the window to the soul or lack of it. Bob is a cheerful, upbeat man, confident in his ability without being an asshole about flossing, and I will always be extremely grateful to him for repairing the damage done to my mouth from years of neglect, candy, drinking, and the occasional long-ago bar fight.

Bob isn't just an artist, though; he's a doctor as well. A very good one, so when he looked at my regular checkup x-rays in the fall of 2017 he saw something that most of his kind would have missed. Actually he didn't really see anything on the x-ray—he just felt that it wasn't right somehow. He poked around in my mouth with that little pointed metal spike and asked if it was painful, which of course it was, because he was poking around in my mouth with a little pointed metal spike. He hemmed and hawed and then decided he wanted me to see his pal Dr. Bustamente. Bob is part of a network of doctors in Beverly Hills who all seem to know one another and are basically rock stars in their field. And they are really like rock stars: they all have motorcycles and guns and it's very expensive to get them to show up.

Dr. Bustamente is a root canal guy, *the* root canal guy, the Meat Loaf of the molar—the Iggy of the incisor—so I trudged over to his office and he took some x-rays but he didn't see anything either, but he poked around with his painful little pointy metal stick and then agreed with Bob that there was something wrong, so he ordered a CAT scan of my head. A painless—except for the cost— procedure that was performed immediately in a scary, dark little room in his suite of offices. Within seconds the colored screen of the fancy, spaceshipish, look-inside-your-head machine lit up with the awful truth.

> *I originally typed* trooth *instead of* tooth *here and spell-check corrected me, but spell-check, while useful, is a fuck-ing humorless bureaucrat with no sense of fun. Still, it must be depressing to have your sole purpose in the uni-verse be pointing out other people's mistakes. Am I right, Internet trolls, gossip columnists, and clergymen?*

Hidden behind the root of a molar was a dark pool of poison and infection that, if not treated as soon as possible, could become a much more serious problem. An abscess that could inflame rapidly and make me very sick indeed. Dr. Bustamente laid out a treatment plan. I needed two surgeries, one to clean out the infection and then a course of antibiotics, and then the repair to the root performed about a month or so later. I agreed, obviously, and a few days later I was headed back to his office for the start of the work, hangry (yes, hangry—fucking relax, spell-check) and thirsty from following the instructions of the anesthesiologist.

Beginning a series of intensive dental work is a bleak enough prospect at any time, but the atmosphere of the world in the winter of 2017/2018 piled misery on my misery like maggots on an old dead goose. Yes, 'twas a bleak Christmas that year, Mr. Scrooge. Kim Jong-un was going to nuke us all, maniacs with automatic weapons seemed to be everywhere, and Harvey Weinstein had recently been outed as a monstrous sexual predator. This in turn had kicked off a flood of similar accusations leading to the #MeToo and #TimesUp campaigns. Whilst undeniably necessary and overdue, these movements had a disturbing side effect, particularly in their early days, of inducing a state of distrust and paranoia in areas where men and women routinely work together. In show business, that's everywhere.

There were multiple daily accusations of horrible crimes or awful harassing behavior by beloved entertainers and respected executives that shocked and appalled everyone, including, it seemed, the beloved entertainers and respected executives, although for different reasons. The atmosphere in the media both social and traditional alternated from righteous indignation to toxic and accusatory. Every crappy gossip blogger wanted to be Ronan Farrow, and it felt like any man was a tweet or a Facebook post away from public shaming and ruin. Like other revolutions it was the best of times, it was the worst of times.

It was the time of the clickbait terror.

Victims of assault and abuse were being believed at last, and a good thing too! But there were some distressing missteps. I thought this at the time but bravely said nothing to avoid being drawn into the fight. Men like me who agreed wholeheartedly with the change that was occurring were reticent to voice any opinion for fear of being accused of mansplaining. Matt Damon, confused and upset by the impending death of his father and with a dud of a movie to promote, stumbled into the public pillory daily for about two weeks by just not knowing when to zip it. As my dear wife occasionally reminds me: "Never miss an opportunity to shut the fuck up."

> *At the time, I toyed with speaking up about my own slight brush with harassment, although ultimately I decided against it. Early on in my career in Hollywood I was propositioned insistently by an actress on a production I worked on. She was far more essential to the project than I was. After I politely declined her increasingly graphic offers of intimacy and she realized I was not being coy but was in fact not interested, she got a bit grumpy and, I think, embarrassed. She suggested to the producers, repeatedly and in no uncertain terms, that I be let go, which would have been a disaster for me because I was flat broke and really needed the job. Thankfully I was kept on because they'd been down that road with her before with her and another actor.*

It was a horrible position to be put in, but it paled in comparison to the stories from the women who were coming forward, so I did shut the fuck up about it then. And I'm glad I did, because nothing would have been gained from shaming this woman who ultimately got herself sorted out, and nothing had actually happened anyway.

And no, it wasn't Betty White, because I'd have done Betty in a heartbeat if she'd offered.

Men were afraid to help, which is, well, unhelpful. The idea of using fear to combat fear seems a little like the notion of arming everybody to fight gun violence. Fear makes people act irrationally. Every man I know was quietly running a mental inventory of his interactions with women. Not just his sex life, but when he might have said something hurtful or demeaning or derogatory to a female colleague. I was concerned because, whilst I am happy to say that my conscience is clear regarding any form of physicality with a woman unless it was specifically asked for in instructional detail, I have made my living for many years telling dirty jokes and saying inappropriate things. Sometimes I have fucked up these jokes or they weren't that good or whoever was hearing them didn't like them, and sometimes all three at the same time. That's a risk you take with jokes. As far as inappropriate things, I may have said them at the wrong time, but if I had said them at the right time they would have been appropriate and would have been far less likely to be funny. It's very difficult to be appropriately inappropriate.

I hope I have never purposefully tried to make someone feel bad about who they are. I hope I've never made a woman—or a

man—feel uncomfortable during an interview on television or radio or anywhere else, for that matter, but to be honest I might have.
I don't remember everything I've said. Luckily the Internet does.
The fucking Internet. The fucking Internet and the motherfucking
gobshite British tabloids. Those dirty scandal sheets that peddle
disgrace and heartache as entertainment and make American gossip sites look like genteel church newsletters. These are the people
who hacked the cell phone of a murder victim to titillate their
desperate mouth-breathing readers. They are the diseased crones
sitting at the foot of the guillotine, waiting to cheer in a lurid,
screaming font as another head drops in the basket. I'm not a fan.

On the morning of the first of my dental surgeries, I Googled
myself, as usual, to see if I was in any sort of trouble. This was a
habit I picked up when I was in late-night television so I'd know
what to be contrite about on that night's show.

> *Occasionally I'd find myself in the doghouse for some stu-*
> *pid comment I'd made the night before. I once had to apol-*
> *ogize to the entire country of Australia for calling their*
> *capital city a shithole. I've never been to Canberra, but*
> *many Australians I've met have told me it is in fact a*
> *shithole, and I think that's the context of what I was saying.*
> *It was during an interview with the Australian actor Guy*
> *Pearce. You can look it up online if you want context, al-*
> *though no one seems to care about context anymore. If*
> *you're an offended Australian, you probably remember.*
> *Either way, I apologize again. I should not have said that*
> *Canberra was a shithole, I should have said it was allegedly*
> *a shithole.*

The first headline that came up that morning was:

Creepy interview resurfaces of Late Late Show *host Craig Ferguson commenting on Meghan Markle's "strangely hairless body."*

From the UK's grimy, muckraking but much-read *Daily Mirror.*

I was horrified. Adrenaline surged through my own strangely hairless body. I knew who Meghan Markle was, of course, because she was everywhere since her engagement to Prince Harry, the reason for this English paper's interest in her. I had interviewed her one night in 2013 when she was one of the cast members of the popular show *Suits,* which I admit—and I admitted to her then—I've never seen. The story cast me in such an appalling light that I was sure that I was about to be outed as the newest sex pest.

First of all, to say that the video had *resurfaced* implied that it had somehow been hidden, probably by me in an attempt to keep my shameful secret. But everything I've ever done on television has been sitting on YouTube for anyone to see for years, usually from the day after it's been broadcast. The whole point of making television is to have people see it.

The *Mirror* story itself took the line that I had been aggressive sexually with Ms. Markle and that I had flirted with her in an inappropriate manner, dismissing her and sexualizing her at every opportunity. The inference was that I should be #MeTooed as being part of the problem. I sounded like a horrible, horrible man, which is something I try not to be.

Obviously I watched the interview again, and while it looks a little tone-deaf in today's climate, I couldn't see anything particularly awful. Just two professional entertainers trying to cobble together an amusing conversation for a late-night TV audience.

The offending observation was early on: I said she was hairless and asked if that was because she was a competitive swimmer, which, as any improviser will tell you, is just an easy lob to get the ball rolling. I admit I asked her if she wanted to do the "smell my finger awkward pause," but I had asked the same thing of hundreds of other guests, women and men (and a horse and a robot skeleton). It was a regular bit on the show. Was I guilty of harassing all of these people? Was I, like the Boston Strangler, unaware of my crimes until confronted with them? I called my lovely but tough-as-nails publicist, Cheryl, and asked if this was something I should worry about.

"No. It's made-up bullshit. You're too boring to be a story," she said kindly.

I read the comments on the newspaper's site. There were only a few, and they all called out the "journalist" as being an idiot and said that there was no scandal to be had. Everyone seemed to agree with Cheryl that this was a nasty example of clickbait using Ms. Markle's name and a hot-button topic in a deeply cynical attempt to draw attention to the website. I Googled the writer of the piece, an unpleasant, manky Australian shit peddler, a fairly common specimen of the tabloid world. Maybe she was from Canberra and was taking revenge for my unkind comments on her fair city. Whatever her motive, if she even thinks deeply enough for that kind of thing, the effect on me was traumatic. The only rest I got that day was the propofol nap in the dental surgery. To make matters worse, the grubby little "neener neener, we saw your wiener" column was written in the ghastly style of pornographic reporting that had infected every media source at the time, not just the tabloids. She used words like "creepy" and "resurfaced" to spice things up and draw in the casual Internet window shopper who may be looking for scandal. Dare I say that her inappropriate remarks made me feel extremely uncomfortable?

> I think it is enormously counterproductive to a healthier sexual climate if crimes and harassment cases are reported in the breathless, erotic novella style that has become fashionable. It plays into the mind-set of the perpetrator. There's nothing sexual for the victim of a so-called sexual assault. That experience belongs to the predator. Call the assault brutal or criminal or disgusting, but calling it sexual in a headline is disingenuous. That's using sex to sell the story, which would imply you concur with the assaulter that there was something sexual happening. Or, more likely, it's letting everyone know you are a semiliterate hack with no journalistic integrity whatsoever—although there is not much shame attached to being that anymore.

Uncomfortable as I was about being vaguely implicated as some kind of loathsome actress-botherer, it was nothing compared to the aftermath of my intense root canal surgery. When I came round, Dr. Bustamente told me that the infection had been much worse than he initially thought. They had managed to get it all out and would be able to save the tooth, but I should expect some pretty intense pain in the next few days. He wanted to give me Percocet, an opioid painkiller that is popular with alcoholics looking to fuck up their lives after long periods of continuous sobriety. I was determined not to use the drug. I'd muscle through on Advil and Tylenol, I told him. He raised his eyebrows and said he'd give me the prescription anyway just in case.

Whatever painkiller had been used in the surgical procedure was still in my system, so I went to bed for the rest of the day, endlessly Googling myself or checking my Twitter feed to see if the *Daily Mirror* had ignited a social media firestorm of derision against me and I had become the next loathed and vilified creep to get his photo posted in the Weinstein Pantheon of Perverts. That ever-growing collection of images of guilty-looking, seedy men that leered out of every website and magazine. The Creep Cavalcade.

The next day the pain came. I lasted about six or seven hours and then I just couldn't take any more. I have a fairly decent threshold for agony—I have some tattoos on some tender places and I went through a three-month bout of shingles by taking Advil and sitting in baths filled with oatmeal (which—weirdly—help a lot but for a long time afterward I smelled like porridge and was followed by hopeful Victorian street urchins).

I had never experienced pain anything like that, though, so Megan filled the prescription. After talking to my sponsor in an anonymous twelve-step program, let's call him John—coincidentally that's his name—I took the Percocet and waited to get high. The high never came. I thought there'd be a rush or a feeling of "coming on," but there was nothing. Just the sweet relief of the pain ebbing away over the next forty-five minutes. I have not been so grateful to pharmaceuticals since my granny gave me

a Mogadon—a super-potent old-people tranq—after a three-day
bout with speed when I was eighteen.

> *The anonymous twelve-step program to which I have long*
> *been a grateful member has a tradition that asks those who*
> *belong to it to maintain a personal anonymity in books and*
> *in the media. I try to respect that as much as I can, but*
> *given that I'm an alcoholic who's been sober for a long time,*
> *you can probably guess what it is.*

I remained vigilant and cautious and careful about the use of
the drug, taking less than prescribed and only when the pain got
too much. I obsessively checked the Internet to see if there was
any traction from the *Mirror* article, but apart from a few gleeful
evil tweets and a little pickup from gossip sites in—of course—
Australia, there wasn't much about me. But by God, there seemed
to be a new accusation and grubby story about a different man
every ten minutes. I fell down a deep, dark Internet hole of following every rumor and insinuation about what seemed an endless
parade of rapists and perverts.

I would be lying if I said I didn't experience some schadenfreude, but the greater feeling was paranoia. Some of the accused
men were vehemently denying the charges made against them,
but the court of public opinion was having none of it. What would
I say if I was falsely accused? Everyone would believe it was true
and there was nothing I could do. There would be no joking about
it. Jokes about sexual harassment were and are considered a form
of sexual harassment. I have a big problem with this. Telling

someone they can't make a joke about something is a sinister tool of fundamentalism. If jokes can be made about death and murder and misery, then they can be made about sexual harassment. They should be good jokes, I agree, clever jokes and not cruel and piling on the problem, but to say there can't be *any at all* is just plain wrong.

Humor is an essential human coping mechanism for dealing with trauma.

A good joke sets the victim free.

I refer you to Roberto Benigni's *La vita è bella* as your homework assignment.

I tried to get off Twitter, which I had had my doubts about for a while anyway. Since the 2016 election, it had become a seething cauldron of name-calling and bitterness, but it seemed to have gotten even worse. Lately, it seemed like everyone was trying to catch everyone else out. I was too paranoid to tweet anything anyway. I threw my phone away and then just continued to Google myself and check my Twitter timeline on my PowerBook whilst pretending to be writing this book.

After a few days I returned to the Dentist to the Stars—Bob Rifkin—because the pain was lasting longer than anyone thought it should. He decided the bite was a little off, drilled the offending molar, and magically—almost immediately—the pain was gone. If I am ever called upon to maul Bob Rifkin in the arena in front of Caesar, I will instead lie down in front of him and let him stroke my lovely mane.

Now that the physical pain was gone, I was free from the Percocet, but its effect lingered. My attendance to the meetings of the anonymous twelve-step group to which I belong had dropped to zero. I was in a stranger mental condition than I had been in for a long, long time. I was now harboring a secret desire to run away to the Mexican town of Juárez—a town I've never been to in my life—and get drunk. My compulsive scouring of the online gossip sites and showbiz trade sites (which were even more frantic) and my devouring of the salacious reports and social media posts of countless occasions of villainy and depravity had led me to believe that the world was as dark and fucked up as it had ever been and the whole thing was going to end at any moment.

I lost all sense of perspective, to say nothing of gratitude. I had no internal equilibrium. I was piping the raw sewage of fear and revulsion into my brain with almost every waking moment. I reached the bottom of the well and began fantasizing about suicide, imagining death as being like the propofol ride I'd experienced during the surgery—blissful nothingness.

There have been few times darker than this in my life, and yet I was almost twenty-six years sober with a family that I love and enough money to keep them comfortable.

As David Byrne so succinctly put it, "Well, how did I get here?"

I'm still not quite sure. I think, like the rest of the world, I was going through a painful but essential transition. I had an infection, unknown to me and undetectable to the untrained eye. It was festering and making me sick. The treatment seemed traumatic and at times unnecessary—I mean, why not just pull the fucking tooth and be done with it.

> *I actually suggested this to everyone around me, but they were all American, and Americans don't really get the concept of tooth-pulling as being an option. In Britain it would*

have been a pair of pliers and a cup of hot, sweet tea and the
whole thing would be over.

Years before, I had heard from someone—again let's call him
John 'cause it's the same guy—the phrase:

"Nothing changes if nothing changes."

I took action. Even though I didn't want to, I returned to the
meetings of the anonymous twelve-step group of which I have
long been a member. I could tell that my kids had noticed I was in
something of a mess, and Megan was in that condition of frustration and concern known as "being married to an alcoholic." I
hadn't been drinking or taking drugs other than prescribed, but I
had lost my way. I was what's referred to in enlightened circles as
"dry drunk." I have to tell you it is nowhere near as much fun as
being wet drunk.

Somehow we got through Christmas with me forcing a smile
as much as I could, and then on January 1 I wished my followers
and my bots on Twitter a happy New Year, left social media, and
cut my news input to two sites. First, the BBC, which while far
from perfect and certainly not above a partisan political stance, is
less inclined to hyperbolic clickbait headlines, and I appreciate
that very much. I also follow the *Glasgow Herald*, but I imagine that
has limited appeal for most of you.

I'm not perfect, of course, as you probably are already aware,
so I still occasionally Google myself, and every now and then
something alarming pops up. Most recently (as of the writing of
this) a heart-stopping piece of clickbait from a website called
TVOvermind that yells: "In the New Age of Sexual Assault Allegations, Watch Craig Ferguson's Talk Show Again."

Holy Mother of God!

The article which follows is actually a positive one about how women are capable of enjoying ribald banter just as much as men, as evidenced on my old late-night show, but to be honest I wish they had gone with a different header. To see your name next to the words *New* and *Sexual Assault Allegations* is no way to start the day!

You may have noticed that there have been posts on my Twitter account since my retirement from social media too. Plugs for my radio show or live dates; probably there will be info about this very book. But in the spirit of full disclosure, you should know that my Twitter account is now monitored by my friend Tomas, the giant Czech hippie vampire who works with me as tour manager and producer of my radio show and stand-up specials. I had him set the parental controls on my phone and computer, and he alone has the passwords.

I couldn't access Twitter even if I wanted to. Unless I ask him for the code, of course, but I won't do that, because I don't want to look weak to the man I had asked to set the parental controls on my phone.

I'm Celtic. We're a paradoxical people.

In paradox there is hope—it might be crazy but it might be true.

It feels wrong but it's right, or maybe the other way round.

I finished the course of antibiotics and returned to Dr. Bustamente for the second surgery. When I was woken from the propofol siesta I knew immediately it was over. There was no pain at all. Not then or later. I took some Advil to be on the safe side, but I needn't have bothered. He really is a very good doctor.

The emotional mindfuck of the dry drunk was over too. I went

back to the meetings and sipped that lousy coffee from foam cups
and listened and talked to those people who drank like me when
they were drinking and thought like me when they were thinking, and I was grateful to be there. Through their perspective, I
regained enough balance to realize that it matters less what some
vicious twerp in a tabloid or on the Internet thinks of me than it
does how I behave. I'm not a saint, but I'm not a fucking sex pest
or a dictator or a mad gunman either. I'm somewhere in between,
like nearly everybody else.

Finding the hidden poison in the root leads to painful and distressing treatment, but painful and distressing treatment leads to
the cure. Action creates results, not thought.

22

Millport

Finally, let me tell you about Great Cumbrae. To the Fergusons of Glasgow, it has as much spiritual significance as Sri Lanka has to a Tamil Buddhist. It is a small, picture-postcard-perfect, rocky, hilly, beachy island off the west coast of Scotland, ideally situated in the firth of the great River Clyde to be protected from the worst rages of Atlantic storms by the much larger Isle of Bute and the Kintyre peninsula. Its hills are covered in lush purple heather or prickly yellow gorse or dark green grass being chomped by chubby, dirty white sheep. There is only one town on the island: Millport. In its heyday between 1875 and 1975, Millport was a mecca for working-class Glaswegians during their annual two-week vacation from the factories and shipyards during the last two weeks of July. It is a miniature hybrid of Coney Island and Brigadoon with a couple of cafés (the Ritz is my favorite—a plate of mushy peas and cup of hot tea, if you're asking), a few hotels, and some wildly eclectic gift shops. In those shops, it is possible to buy big plastic buckets and spades to make sand castles, or a souvenir snow globe, or a magic trick or toy bagpiper in a plastic tube, or those strange wee Victorian dolls so beloved by cat ladies. You could get an ABBA or Bay City Rollers or Joy Division T-shirt, or some fake dog poo, or joke vomit, or a Whoopee cushion, or a pound of boiled sweeties in a paper bag. In one of these wondrous emporiums, Mapes, it is possible to rent a bike. Any type of bike you need, as long as it has pedals—kids' tricycles, big Mary Poppins things with wicker baskets on the front, tandems, and unicycles. All at a very reasonable hourly rate. When I was a child Millport was our Disneyland, the happiest place on earth.

When I was very young my father would take my brother and sisters and me to the tide pools on the rocks near the beach. We'd look for limpets and sea anemones and crabs, being very careful on the bright green seaweed, which was as slippery as show business. My father would lift up heavy rocks and, to our delight, all the little critters underneath would scuttle off in panic. Occasionally there would be a large rock crab that my dad would carefully pick up from behind its claws and he'd let us look closely at it, its alien legs and pincers waving in fury. When we'd been sufficiently creeped out, he'd gently return the manic, outraged crustacean to a nearby pool and we'd watch fascinated until it scuttled off to a new hiding place. I was in awe of my father's bravery and expertise with these animals and thought he was wasting his talents in the post office. He could have been a professional crab handler. He assured me that was not something he was interested in.

The island is eight miles or so in its circumference, and the mark of adulthood was being able to ride a rented cycle around its flat coastal road. This is pretty safe because there are very few motorized vehicles. They have to get there by boat and they don't really have anywhere to go once they arrive. I first made the trip when I was about nine years old and it seemed endless and difficult and exciting, although these days it seems short and often agreeable. Like life.

There is a small park in the town of Millport called the

Garrison. I don't know why it's called that; I suspect soldiers may have been based there at some point or perhaps it's where Mr. Keillor had the idea for *A Prairie Home Companion*, but either way it is where all the action was during the summer. There were trampolines provided for free by the local council. Six of them stretched across the ground over what looked like fresh graves. Youngsters would line up for their chance to show their acrobatic skills or more likely chip a tooth or break a bone on the stone edging that the rusty springs were hooked onto. There was also the municipal "bathing pond," which was a rather grand title for a two-foot-deep concrete-lined pit that was filled with hyperchlorinated water, paint chips, and pee. If the air temperature crept above sixty degrees the pond would be jam-packed with enormously excited tubby children, turning it into some awful, living, breathing soup. The sensation of being in there was less like swimming and more like being a participant in a smelly, damp riot.

To the rear of the Garrison were "the shows"—a little merry-go-round, some rides and swings, and an amusement arcade, which consisted of a half-dozen pinball machines from the 1950s and a couple of other bright-colored machines that were purpose-built to steal coins from children. There was a bingo hall where pensioners sat with their tiny wee pencils in their arthritic claws hoping that their numbers would be called by the spivvy-looking bloke with Brylcreemed hair and a cad's mustache. They could win a stuffed toy or a carton of cigarettes or, twice a day, the big prize, a bottle of Famous Grouse Scotch Whisky.

This entire showbiz empire was owned and run by one family—the Newtons, who would take turns working in a glass booth in the center of the arcade to keep an eye on the customers

and dispense change to those who needed it. Jimmy Newton, the
patriarch of the family, was a tough-looking balding gent who was
to become my first boss. When I was fourteen years old I was
whining to my parents about having no money to play pinball or
try out the new air hockey table that seemed to be a magnet for
every good-looking girl on the island. My father suggested that if
I wanted to have money, maybe I should get a job, and he told me
to ask Mr. Newton if he needed any help. I plucked up the courage
and approached the taciturn carney in his glass cell, a scene that
was to be duplicated in cinema many years later when Clarice
Starling approaches Hannibal Lecter for the first time in *Silence of
the Lambs.*

"Excuse me, Mr. Newton, do you need anybody to work here?"

He sucked hard on his cigarette, then looked me up and down
through the exhaled smoke. I don't know how I could tell, but he
was definitely guessing my weight. To my utter astonishment he
said I had a job. I could work the swingboats. The swingboats!
This was unbelievable; the swingboats were Millport's Studio 54.
The hot destination for the teenage fast set. They were boat-shaped
two-seaters in which two people sat facing each other and pulled
ropes to draw themselves to the desired height. Boys would take
their dates on them and pull the ropes as hard as they could. The
boats didn't spin, but they would hurtle higher and higher into the
air, making the girls scream. Girls would go on them together in
order to be visible to the potential suitors who would prowl the
fairground like hungry jackals. Like in any courtship ritual, the
boys were always much more afraid than the girls. Boys never
went on the swingboats together; this would be an admission of
homosexuality, which could result in derision or even violent

attention from other boys. My job was to collect the fees and push the boats to get them started and then when the allotted time was up, to grab the boat and bring it to a stop. It requires a decent amount of body weight to stop a hurtling swingboat. That's why Mr. Newton gave me the coveted gig in the first place. My tubbiness was exactly what was required.

I met every kid on the island and earned one pound and sixty-five pence for a ten-hour day with a half hour for lunch. This was probably against the child labor laws even then, but I loved that job. I will never be as rich or as famous as I was in the summer of 1976. If it hadn't been for Jimmy Newton I would never have gotten into show business.

In 2005 my father was dying and I was traveling back to Scotland as much as I could to be with him. I suggested that we go to Millport for a day out and though he loved the idea, on the day we planned he was just too sick and tired. He told me I should take a break and go on my own with Milo, who was only four years old at the time. We drove to Largs and took the ferry to Great Cumbrae, and when we got to Millport, to my astonishment, Jimmy Newton was still there. Still taking money in the little glass booth. The rides were much fancier and there were no swingboats, but he was still the same man, a little older and grayer but still impressive-looking, although not nearly as frightening as I remembered him. As Milo jumped around on the big bright bouncy castle I went over and reintroduced myself. He recognized me because the Scottish press had been full of me getting the job as host of *The Late Late Show* on CBS, but I could tell he had no memory of me as the tubby stopper of the boats. I told him how transformative an experience it had been for me to work for him, and he smiled and said that he would be happy to give me my old job back at the same daily rate. I wish that somehow we could have made that work.

I have returned to Millport time and time again since I was a kid. I think because for me it is infused with a magical happiness. The fondest memories of my childhood are from there.

I ran there in the last days of my drinking in order to try to find some solace, but it was ineffectual as a cure since it has alcohol available to those who need or want it. I think that's when I really knew the game was up. If you go to Millport and you still feel like shit, then it's you. You are the problem.

After I had been to rehab in 1992, I returned to Glasgow to be given yet another second chance by BBC Scotland. The show I did for them was called *2000 Not Out*. It was nobody's idea of a creative or ratings success, but I was on time for filming or rehearsal every day and didn't smell like pee or whisky when I showed up. I was pleased to be back in Scotland but a little scared of going out anywhere after work lest I somehow be struck drunk. I spent a lot of time with the great and much-missed Scottish actor Sean Scanlan.

Sean was a legend in Scottish theater, as an actor of astonishing power and presence and, until 1991, a spectacularly self-destructive alcoholic. He used to drink in the pub in Glasgow where I was a barman and I had seen him in his cups. It was a sight to behold: a fat, red, shouty giant who seemed to fall over every time he stood up. When he disappeared from the scene I naturally assumed he was dead. I hardly recognized him when we bumped into each other on the street in London a few days after I got out of the treatment center. He looked twenty years younger and forty pounds lighter and as luck would have it was also headed back to Scotland to do a job.

Sean and I spent a lot of time together over the next few months, sitting in cafés or going for curries and learning how to be in Glasgow without being wasted all the time. I think we were both shocked at how cool and friendly and interesting a city it was. On the weekend I got my driving license back, I suggested we take my ancient Mercedes "doon the watter" to Millport.

We smoked cigarettes outside the Ritz Café and strolled along the promenade like a nice respectable gay couple on a day out. It was stunning weather and I decided I wanted to go for a run round the island. I asked Sean if he wanted to go with me and he said, "Fuck no, dear boy. I'd rather cut off my hand."

He sat on a bench at the pier, rolling and smoking cigarettes and reading *The Varieties of Religious Experience* by William James while I put on the shorts and T-shirt and sneakers that I kept in the car (I carried a running kit around like I used to carry miniature bottles of booze) and started out clockwise round the island. I never run anticlockwise—*widdershins*—lest I summon the devil.

I ran past the cafés and the Garrison and the pubs and the rock painted like a crocodile, imaginatively called Crocodile Rock. I ran past Kames Bay, the large open sandy beach where when I was fifteen a bikini-clad Big Margaret McCafferty had asked me to rub suntan oil on her back and legs and I was almost rendered unconscious by the conflicting emotions of desire and terror and shame.

I listen to music when I run. It helps the meditation. I was listening to Brian Eno that day, an album called *Before and After Science*. Eno is the composer of the musical score to my life. The first album I ever bought was his *Here Come the Warm Jets* when I was in my early teens, although to be honest I think that was as much about the small picture of a naked lady's bottom on the cover as it was the music.

The way I see it there is no point in drinking unless you're going to get drunk, and there's no point in listening to music unless it's loud, so my Discman—it's 1992—was cranked.

Side one, track two. "Backwater."

> *We're sailing at the edges of time.*
> *We're drifting at the water line.*

The obvious problem with running outside whilst listening to music very loudly on headphones is that it is impossible to hear danger approaching. I didn't know it was hatching time for the oystercatchers that make their nests on the shore of the island, and even if I did I had no idea how aggressive and territorial these birds are, especially when their nests are packed with babies. I didn't hear the mother caw and screech as I ran too close to her squeaking and tweeting children. She must have been very angry, because even though I was twenty times her size, she swooped down and hit me in the back of the head. I don't know if it was with her beak or her feet or a billy club she kept hidden under her feathers, but what I do know was that one minute I was running, then I got a solid blow to the head, and seconds later I was sprawled out on the deck like Sonny Liston after a few rounds with Ali. Both my knees were grazed, same with my hands. I was banged up but not too badly. The poor Discman was a goner, though. Its innards were scattered across the road like a yard sale of spare electronics.

I got up and watched the oystercatcher hurtle herself wildly

toward the heavens, screeching her mad cry of victory. I inspected
my injuries and though they stung they were nothing compared to
the other, deeper scars from recent battles. I took the ruined Discman and dropped it into a nearby trash can. I dropped the disc
in too; it was scratched beyond repair. It was time for me to run
on alone. To hear the soundtrack of reality.

The sea was Celtic green, calm and deep and resting between
storms. The waves and gulls and wind made a more subtle ambient soundtrack. The bluest sky in history accentuated its infinite
clarity by building a motionless bulging white tower of cumulus
on the distant horizon directly in my path. The ineffable beauty of
the world filled me with a dizzying sense of gratitude.

In my memory now I still do as I did that day. I brush off the
loose stones and debris that attached to me after my fall, and this
can't be true but it is. In the clouds ahead I see your face and the
faces of our children and I smile and then I roar with delight as I
run as fast as I can toward you.

23

Margaret

She was dancing almost before she was walking. In the long winter nights before the television or movies, the crofters would gather round peat fires in their damp turf-roofed cottages and sip the *uisge beatha* and tell stories and sing songs. Everyone had a party piece, a small entertainment they could perform to contribute to the fight against the deep depression of the dark. Margaret was cuddly as a three-day lamb, a shock of blond hair gifted from a long-dead Viking invader and eyes as green and blue as the kelp. Her cheeks reddened as she threw herself at her routine and they all adored her. They reveled in the profound dignity and seriousness with which the striking tubby child performed her jig, her arms rigid by her sides, her tiny face all grim determination as her wee legs kicked as high as her chubby frame would allow. Her parents and her aunts and uncles and cousins and friends and even the minister—if it wasn't a Sunday—all laughed until the tears rolled down their cheeks. They clapped along in time to the fiddle, whooping encouragement to their own precocious and serious tiny star. They were her first audience and she had often imagined their faces out there in the darkness beyond the spotlights of grander stages.

She missed the islands when her family left, but she understood the realities of it. She was almost twelve years old and Queen

Victoria had died and it seemed the world was changing. The winters were so harsh in the Hebrides and her uncle had written from Glasgow telling of a place of industry and wealth where a skilled carpenter like her father could prosper, or at least not worry about feeding his family. Like many crofting families they headed to the big city in pursuit of a better life.

Her grandmother refused to leave with them, preferring to see out her days where she had lived them. She told them she was too old to learn a new language. Margaret's heart broke the day they left, and she wept long after the ferry pulled away from the pier, leaving the old woman to be consumed by the morning fog.

Her grandmother had the soul of a poet and was her introduction to the magic of the world. She brushed Margaret's hair one hundred times every night and told her stories of the sea nymphs and monsters and faeries and ghosts. On the warm spring mornings, they played the game of trying to see the spirits in the fog. Her grandmother told her that the sea mist was more than it seemed; it wasn't just the low clouds rolling in from the ocean but also the blurring of the space between the worlds. Between the living and the dead, the true and the false, the remembered and the forgotten. Her grandmother told her that if she looked hard enough she would see the face of the man she would marry. Margaret had tried so hard to see all these things but never once did she get the slightest glimpse. On the ferry, it just looked cold and scary and bleak until eventually it had swallowed the woman.

The family struggled in Glasgow at first, not least learning to speak English, which seemed to be a much more complicated language than their native Gaelic. Her father had been unable to find work right away and almost fell into the trap of drinking to forget his troubles, but he was saved by a fiery and enthusiastic minister of the kirk, a Highland émigré who gave him a paid job working on the church buildings on weekdays and forced him to his knees for somber Protestant thankfulness on a Sunday. Her brothers were too young to work, but Margaret and her mother found jobs in the steamie—Glasgow slang for the laundry—where they'd fold and press clothes and sheets for the wealthier customers who could afford to have someone do that job for them. No one had washing machines at home—very few people even had inside toilets—so the steamie was not only a place of work but a place where the women could meet and talk and socialize. It had the added bonus of being free of men who, in this town, were often dangerous or drunk or both.

The dark tenement where they slept and ate was shared with countless other families. It was noisy and smelly and cramped and cold, and Margaret much preferred being at work, which was noisy and smelly and cramped but hot and full of vibrant, funny women. She loved how it sent huge billowing clouds of condensation out into the street, frightening the horses and irritating the tram drivers on St. Georges Road. Margaret pulled her weight and did her job and lived for Saturday afternoons when she would have half a day to herself and she could go to the Empire.

The Glasgow Empire was a music hall, a vaudeville house, a palace of entertainment. To Margaret and thousands of other working-class people it was an oasis of fantasy and laughter in an otherwise grim and difficult existence. She sat in the stalls of the fabulously ornate and vulgar theater with the other young women, or occasionally with a twitching and uncomfortable young man who her father deemed worthy enough to escort her. She laughed with the comedians and sang with the singers and marveled at the acrobats and envied the dancing girls. It never occurred to her that it would be a world which she could enter, not until the day she was handed a flyer by a shifty-looking old geezer who waited outside the theater accosting young women and offering them a chance to audition for the chorus line.

She passed the audition and was offered a permanent job on the chorus before she mentioned anything to her parents. By this time, she was seventeen but they were, predictably, against her taking the position. Like many provincial people, they equated performing to be synonymous with a louche and wanton lifestyle—which to be fair it often is—but after spirited fights and dire threats they eventually came round, and Margaret dug into the grueling schedule of three shows a day, six days a week.

She thrived in the chorus; young and fit and beautiful, she drew the eye. Her energy and vivacity forced her front and center before long. This of course can be a very dangerous position, especially for a young woman, but Margaret was possessed by a lively intelligence and she kept the predators at bay by a mixture of strength and manners learned from her mother and grandmother. That's not to say she was a saint; as time passed she had occasionally had passionate affairs with other performers, mostly men who were so self-involved that they wouldn't get all doe-eyed about her just because of sex.

By the time the Great War broke out in 1914 she actually had her name on the billboard outside the theater. It was in small type at the bottom, but nevertheless a big thrill for her and the family that she still lived with in the dark tenement.

The days she spent dancing in Glasgow were some of the happiest in her life. Perhaps not altogether the happiest, since there were deeper pleasures ahead, but she never forgot the sheer joy and vivacity of those times.

The war changed everything, of course. The women went to work and the men went to die. She lost both of her brothers and her father in the same day—the second battle of Ypres—Passchendaele—in 1917. They were all together when their regiment, the Argyll and Sutherland Highlanders, was shelled. Her mother seemed to take a sliver of comfort from the fact that they had gone together, but Margaret never saw anything in it but terrible and pointless waste. Her mother died, essentially of a broken heart, before the armistice in November the following year, as much a victim of the German mortar as the rest of her family.

Margaret was offered a job in London, and she took it. Six days a week but only two shows a day in the chorus at the Hackney Empire, a big-time vaudeville house in the East End. She fell into her life there with another Scottish girl she had traveled south with.

She was almost thirty before she met and married Alfonse Francitti and moved to Torino in northern Italy. Alfonse had not seen her dance, did not know she danced, until after they had tea together in a tiny café just off Tottenham Court Road. He had stopped her in the street as she'd come out of Selfridges, where she'd been to get a fancy scarf to send to her ancient grandmother who was still perched on her rock in the North Atlantic, picking at shellfish and casting bones in the sand.

"Excuse me?" he said.

He was older than her but handsome in the classic dark-eyed Italian manner. Impeccably dressed, of course.

"Yes?" she said.

"I am not from here and I am lost. Can you help me?"

"Depends. What are you looking for?"

"My new wife."

"What does she look like?"

"You, I hope."

She rolled her eyes but it made her laugh, and she had a little time and agreed to have tea with him.

It turned out that he was not at all what she had expected. He was a widowed doctor with a four-year-old son who was only in London for a medical conference. He had been to the department store to buy a present for his little boy, who was being looked after by his grandmother in Torino while he was away. It quickly became evident that his bold and convoluted approach to her in the street was wildly out of character. As the years passed he couldn't really explain it himself, but he just was thankful that for once in his life he had succumbed to an impetuous urge. He was, normally, a most measured and rather shy man.

They talked and she invited him to the show. They quickly fell in love the way people sometimes do, and she left the stage and married him and moved to Italy, surpassing the obstacles put in their way by her profession and their opposing religions. Margaret became a Catholic to appease his family, but she never really bought into all that nonsense, not in her heart. She did love the pageantry and ceremony of it, eventually finding it comforting.

She helped him raise the little boy and had two children of her own. They lived happily for a time in Torino, but they loathed and feared the rise of fascism in Europe and immigrated to America in the early 1930s, when doing such a thing was still possible.

They settled in a small town in upstate New York, where Alfonse practiced medicine and Margaret, between raising the children and running their home, studied at night school to gain her bachelor's degree in journalism. She began writing for the local paper. She wrote very well, covering the war and its aftermath. Although she received fancy job offers to go to Manhattan, she stayed in the suburbs, preferring the speed of life there.

Then something happened to her that no one expected, least of all Margaret.

Suddenly she was old.

The children left and had some of their own. Alfonse grew so old that one day he fell asleep and never woke up. Like a massive and not altogether unwelcome change in the weather, death's prospect began its quiet discordant hymn.

She did not want to die in America, much to the annoyance of her children, who were now busy and fussy adults. They fought with her and threatened and pleaded and warned, but she was a fierce Hebridean at the end of a long life, and she was still bright-eyed and intense and smarter than them. She remained unafraid, so she once again followed her old heart.

"America is a country of the young," she told them. "I have to go home."

She sold the little house that she raised them in and bought a flat in Glasgow in the same building she'd moved into as a child all those years ago. The building was old and crumbling like her, but she kept the public stairwell clean with a mop and a bucket of soapy water that she doused it with every day. The winters passed and she survived like the reaper had forgotten her, but of course the reaper never forgets.

The young people who had taken over the neighborhood were polite and kind to her even though they dressed like lunatics with their shirts made of plastic bags and safety pins through their ears and noses. Their music was loud and brash and they were nervous and jumpy, but she adored them. They were young Glaswegian artists, as she had been.

There were so many Italians in Glasgow, it made it even better. Families that immigrated or the descendants of prisoners of war who had remained in the town after the guns had stopped. She didn't have too many friends there now but she spoke fluent Italian, so she was treated like a beloved aged relative in the Equi café in Sauchiehall Street, a short walk from her flat. Art students from the local school gathered there to drink cappuccinos and assess each other's black clothing. She was invisible to all but the most talented of them. She smiled at their youth, their optimism, and their sincerity. It warmed her like the peat fires of her childhood.

She had a television and a telephone, and every Sunday she called her daughter in California. She would make a special call the next day, even though it was only Wednesday, so that they could watch the royal wedding together and talk about the dress.

She was tired that night, though. Too much pasta and a big glass of red wine. Antonio, the son of the café owner, escorted her home as his father had insisted and made sure she was safely locked up for the night before heading off to see his girlfriend.

She combed her long white hair one hundred times and lay down on the cool clean sheets to dream again of Italy and America and London and the Highlands.

She found herself outside on the dark wet street. Although she was wearing only her nightgown she didn't feel cold. She heard a noise, young people laughing and careening home from a bar, no doubt. She turned her head and saw me and Davie and Jacqui and Tricia heading back from the Hellfire Club studio, where Tricia's band had been rehearsing. I faced her for a moment but I didn't see her.

I see her now, though. She is magnificent. Her skin glows with radiant health like it did on the nights she danced at the Empire. Her eyes flash with her astounding visceral intellect. She looks toward St. Georges Road where the steamie used to be and sees the ghost clouds of white that billow from its long ago doors. After all this time, she finally sees the faces in the mist. The man she married and her grandmother and mother and her father and her brothers. She sees the face of the shy young woman who will become a princess tomorrow. She sees the teenage Alison who no longer is doomed and she sees the funny and handsome American boy who had AIDS. She sees my parents and your dad.

She smiles and then runs as fast as she can toward them.

ACKNOWLEDGMENTS

The temptation when writing acknowledgments for a book of this sort is to simply thank everyone you can remember. The people who were nice and the people who were not, they all contribute to memory and therefore have played a part.

But the stories are only memories unless they are told.

These are the people that help me tell my stories and to whom I am deeply grateful.

John Naismith, who consistently and cheerfully saves me from the ravages of self-obsession. The type of comrade who shows up whether it's a foxhole or a parade. Thanks, pal.

Thanks also to my agent Nancy Josephson, a great agent and great friend.

Cheryl Snow and Harold Brown, the only two lawyers in the world that I like.

My trusted confidante and part-time spiritual advisor David Leventhal, who saves me from my financial incompetence.

Cuban dynamo Haydee Campos, who runs the ship and makes sure the lights stay on.

The remarkable Cheryl Maisel, who patiently manages my discomfort with visibility.

The quietly tenacious Mel Berger, who bolstered and believed in the idea.

Thanks to the dashing Czech Tomas Zakopal, who somehow manages to find order in the chaos, and thank you, "Malibu" Joe Bolter, for creative partnership and the reminder that Californians can be cool.

A deep bow of gratitude to the astoundingly clear-headed and talented Jill Schwartzman, who sanded and varnished and edited and bullied (kindly) and made this book much better than it would have been without her.

Thank you to my mother-in-law Linda Cunningham and my brother-in-law Ian Cunningham, who show up and help every single time.

Also, big ups to Bill Wilson for dropping the dimes in the Mayflower and to Bob Smith for giving him fifteen minutes. Thanks to all of their friends too.

There are also those people without whom there is no point in telling a story or doing anything else.

My True Loves:

Milo Hamish Ferguson,

Liam James Ferguson,

and, of course,

Megan.